OUT OF THE ORCHARD

OUT OF THE
ORCHARD
Recipes for Fresh Fruit from the Sunny Okanagan
JULIE VAN ROSENDAAL
TouchWood
Editions

To the growers and their families who produce real food—in BC and across Canada

CONTENTS

INTRODUCTION

I grew up in Alberta, spending most of my summers, as so many Albertans do, in the BC interior, soaking in the sun and playing in the lakes of the Okanagan Valley. The combination of climate and terroir is not only ideal for summer vacations, but for growing some of the best tree fruit in the world.

Almost year-round, tree fruits from BC show up in my kitchen. Juicy cherries, apricots, peaches and plums explode with the taste of summer, and in the fall and winter I can't get enough crisp apples (both sweet and tart) and perfumed pears. They all inspire me to bake cakes, pies and preserves, but also find their way into salads and savoury dishes, providing that perfect element of flavour, sweetness, acidity and crunch. With so much inspiration to draw from, a cookbook was inevitable.

On the following pages you'll find some of my favourite things to do with Okanagan tree fruit, from classic pies to cobblers and cakes, salads and preserves to soups and stews. Every juicy fruit brings a little bit of that summer sunshine into my kitchen, and I hope to pass it on to yours.

ABOUT BC TREE FRUITS

Fruit has been a part of the Okanagan Valley since before anyone can remember. Indigenous peoples picked wild crabapples, strawberries, thimbleberries and pin cherries before European settlers showed up in the early 1800s with new grafts stashed away in their covered wagons. By the end of the 19th century, orchards were growing all over the Okanagan and had moved beyond apples to pears, peaches, plums, apricots and cherries.

The BC Tree Fruits Cooperative was established in 1936 as a means for locals to help each other market and transport their fruit; today it's owned by over 500 grower families dedicated to nurturing the land and their orchards. (It's a true co-operative: the growers actually own the packing houses and their associated assets.) Tree fruit is a big industry in British Columbia, generating $130 million in revenue, contributing $900 million in economic activity and employing 1,500 people. BC Tree Fruits growers, recognized as leaders in the adaptation of modern technology, are a diverse group; many grew up on their farms, while others came from across the country, continent or ocean and were so wowed by the beauty of BC's interior that they were inspired to stay and grow food.

And I'm glad they did.

APPLES 101

There are over 8000 varieties of apple in the world, and over a dozen popularized in the BC interior, most harvested in late fall. While some are more familiar than others, all have their own texture and flavour profile and are worth a try. When baking pies and cakes, I like to use a variety, rather than just stick with one type of apple, which tends to result in one-dimensional baked goods. Whatever you choose, apples are best stored in the fridge—they'll last up to 10 times longer when refrigerated—and wait to wash them just before eating, under running water.

Here's an introduction to the most common apple varieties, and what they're best used for. When in doubt, let your taste buds decide—they're rarely wrong.

ROYAL GALA

Galas are one of the most popular of the BC Tree Fruits family—crisp, firm, bright red and yellow and smaller than most with a thin skin, it's a sweet apple that originated in New Zealand and is a cross between a Golden Delicious and the lesser-known Kidd's Orange Red. In the kitchen, Galas are perfect for pies and baking, and break down well into applesauce. Their small size also makes them ideal for dicing into a salad.

AMBROSIA

Ambrosias are new but popular apples, discovered by growers in the interior of BC in the 1990s as a chance seedling. No one knows its parentage, but the original orchard was full of Jonagolds. Similar in shape to a Yellow Delicious in shades of red and yellow with a pink blush, it's a large, crisp, honey-scented apple that doesn't oxidize (turn brown) as quickly as other varieties once cut, making them perfectly suited to salads, sauces and slicing for cheese platters, fondue and lunchboxes. Sweet-tart and flavourful, they're wonderful in pies and baked goods, too.

RED DELICIOUS

Dating back to the 1880s, Red Delicious are among the most common for eating out of hand. Sweet, crunchy and mellow, they don't hold their shape very well when cooked, so are best eaten raw.

MCINTOSH

Round and green with bright red cheeks, Macs are crunchy and tart, and smaller in size than other varieties. Their flavour makes them a good choice for pie baking, but they tend to break down more than others and are so juicy, you'll need to use a thickener, such as flour. They're best known for the pink-hued applesauce they produce.

JONAGOLD

Larger than most apples, Jonagolds are a cross between Golden Delicious and Jonathan apples. They're firm, crisp, crunchy and sweet and hold their shape when baked, making them perfect for pies.

BRAEBURN

The slightly oval, red and green Braeburn stores well, maintaining its sweet-tart flavour and firm, juicy flesh. They're delicious eating apples and roast well with meats; they're also delicious in pies and other baked goods.

FUJI

With Japanese origins, the Fuji is a cross between a Red Delicious and a lesser-known variety called Ralls Janet. It's larger than most, super sweet with red stripes over a yellow-green background and firm, crunchy flesh. They're excellent for eating out of hand, roasted with meats and in baking and desserts, as they hold their shape well.

GOLDEN DELICIOUS

Pale yellow with a mellow honey flavour, the Golden Delicious is most often eaten raw, although its sweetness makes it ideal for desserts. They break down more easily than other apples, making them perfect for sauce as well.

SPARTAN

The Spartan was the first new breed of apple created by the Pacific Agri-food Research Centre in Summerland, BC. It's smaller than most apples, sweet with deep red skin, snowy-white flesh and a slightly softer interior. They're a great multi-purpose apple, ideal for baking, salads, and eating out of hand.

PINK LADY

Sweet-tart Pink Ladies are crisp and intensely flavourful, with a brighter pink blush than other varieties. They're delicious for snacking, perfect for salads, and their flavour carries well in baked goods and savoury dishes.

NICOLA

Large, sweet and crisp, the Nicola was cultivated locally using natural methods. It has a cherry red blush over a greenish yellow backdrop and a long, elegant stem. It also boasts an outstanding shelf life: up to five months without losing texture or juiciness. It's a perfect multi-purpose apple, delicious in salads, sauces and baked goods, as well as eaten out of hand.

SUNRISE

One of the first varieties to be harvested each year, the Sunrise is a product of the Pacific Agri-food Research Centre in Summerland, BC. They're harvested in August, prompting some to call them "summer apples". Sunrise are excellent all-purpose apples, perfect for eating on their own or for use in pies, baking and sauces.

GRANNY SMITH

Best known as a baking apple, the green Granny Smith is very tart and less sweet than other apples, making them more of an acquired taste for eating out of hand. They don't oxidize as quickly as other apples, which paired with their tartness and crunch makes them great in salads—they're also delicious in pies and other baked goods, as the added sugar makes them sweeter.

HONEYCRISP

A cross between a Macoun and Honey Gold, the Honeycrisp is a large, extraordinarily crisp, honey-scented apple that's delicious on its own as well as in salads, sauces and baked goods.

BREAKFAST

apple pie steel-cut oats

1 cup (250 mL) steel-cut oats
2 cups (500 mL) apple cider
2 cups (500 mL) milk or water
1 apple or pear, cored and chopped
½ tsp (2 mL) cinnamon or a cinnamon stick
Pinch salt
Milk, brown sugar, and toasted nuts, for serving

There is something to be said for waking up in the morning to a cinnamon-scented kitchen and a bowl of warm oatmeal, ready to go. Quantity-wise, doing it in the slow cooker might seem like a lot—but it's perfect when the extended family gathers for brunch. If there aren't that many people at the breakfast table, leftovers can be refrigerated (or frozen) and reheated all week long. And if you have more to feed, the recipe can easily be doubled. If you like, add some ground ginger along with the cinnamon, or a couple of star anise.

Spray the bowl of a slow cooker with nonstick spray and add the oats, cider, milk or water, apple or pear, cinnamon, and salt; stir to combine. Cover and set on low for 4–6 hours. (The slow cooker should turn off in the night and keep the oatmeal warm until you wake up.)

Serve warm topped with milk, brown sugar, and toasted nuts.

SERVES 4–6

apple bourbon sticky buns

DOUGH:

- ½ cup (125 mL) warm water
- 1 Tbsp (15 mL) active dry yeast
- ½ cup (125 mL) sugar
- 1 cup (250 mL) milk, warmed
- 2 large eggs
- 5 cups (1.25 L) all-purpose flour, divided
- ½ cup (125 mL) butter, cut into pieces
- 1 tsp (5 mL) salt

TOPPING:

- ½ cup (125 mL) butter
- 1 cup (250 mL) packed brown sugar
- ⅓ cup (85 mL) golden syrup, corn syrup, or honey
- ¼ cup (60 mL) bourbon, apple cider, or water

FILLING:

- ¼ cup (60 mL) butter, melted
- 1 cup (250 mL) dark brown sugar
- 2 tsp (10 mL) cinnamon
- 1 large or 2 small tart apples, cored and finely chopped

A good sticky bun is the best breakfast item ever invented. Add tart apples and a splash of bourbon to the mix for something really over the top.

To make the dough, put the warm water in a large bowl (or the bowl of your stand mixer) and sprinkle with the yeast and a pinch of the sugar. Let stand 5 minutes or until foamy.

In a small bowl, mix the warm milk and eggs together with a fork. Add to the yeast mixture along with 3 cups (750 mL) of the flour and the remaining sugar; mix until well blended and sticky. Add the butter and remaining flour and stir or beat with the dough hook attachment of your stand mixer until you have a soft, sticky dough. Remove from the bowl and knead for about 8 minutes until smooth and elastic. (Alternatively, knead using the dough hook of your stand mixer.) It will still be slightly tacky. Place back in the bowl, cover with a tea towel, and let rise in a warm place for an hour or until doubled in bulk.

To make the topping, combine the butter, brown sugar, syrup or honey, and bourbon, cider, or water in a small saucepan and bring to a simmer. Stir until the butter is melted, then pour over the bottom of two buttered pie plates, 9-inch (23 cm) cake pans, or 8- × 8-inch (20 × 20 cm) pans.

Divide the dough in half, and on a lightly floured surface, roll each piece into a rectangle about 10 × 15 inches (25 × 38 cm) and ¼ inch (6 mm) thick. Brush each piece with half the melted butter and sprinkle with brown sugar and cinnamon; smooth the sugar to evenly distribute it with your hand. Sprinkle with the chopped apples.

Continued on page 19

Continued from page 16

Starting on a long side, roll the dough up into a log. Using a serrated knife, cut the log crosswise into thirds, then cut each piece into thirds; this is easier than eyeballing it to get 9 even pieces. Place cut side up into the pans, setting one in the middle and the rest around it, or in the case of a square pan, in 3 rows of 3. Cover with a tea towel and let rise for another hour or until doubled in bulk. (If you're making them the night before, cover and place in the fridge for a slow rise; take them out and leave them on the countertop for 30 minutes or so before baking.)

When you're ready to bake, preheat the oven to 350°F (180°C). Put a baking sheet on the rack underneath (to catch any drips) and bake for 30–40 minutes until deep golden. Let cool for 5–10 minutes, then invert onto a plate while still warm.

MAKES 1½ DOZEN BUNS

apple, pear, or stone fruit dutch baby

SAUTÉED FRUIT:
- 1 Tbsp (15 mL) canola oil
- 2 Tbsp (30 mL) butter
- 2 apples, pears, or peaches, cored or pitted and sliced
- 2 Tbsp (30 mL) brown sugar, pure maple syrup, or honey
- Pinch cinnamon

PANCAKE:
- 3 large eggs
- ¾ cup (185 mL) milk
- 1 tsp (5 mL) vanilla
- ¾ cup (185 mL) all-purpose flour

There are two ways you can make a Dutch baby, which is like an eggy puffed pancake: by pouring the batter over sautéed fruit in the pan, then baking it, or pouring the batter into a hot, empty pan, which will allow it to puff up more dramatically; you can then fill it with your choice of fruit. Apples or pears sautéed in butter and sugar make a classic Dutch baby, or try wedges of fresh or caramelized peaches or apricots, chopped plums, or pitted cherries.

Preheat the oven to 450°F (230°C).

In a heavy, ovenproof skillet (cast iron is ideal), heat the oil and butter over medium-high heat. When the foam subsides, sauté the apples, pears, or peaches for 3–4 minutes, until they start to soften and turn golden. Sprinkle with the sugar (or syrup or honey) and cinnamon and cook until the fruit starts to caramelize.

Meanwhile, whisk together the eggs, milk, and vanilla, then whisk in the flour.

If you like, pour the batter over the apples in the skillet and put it in the oven. Otherwise, remove the apples from the skillet, pour in the batter, and put it into the oven.

Bake for 20–25 minutes, until the pancake is puffed and golden. Cut it into wedges and serve warm, sprinkled with icing sugar, if you like, and topped with the fruit (if it's not baked inside) and a drizzle of maple syrup.

SERVES 4

cinnamon pear pancakes

- 2 cups (500 mL) all-purpose flour, or a combination of flours
- 2 tsp (10 mL) baking powder
- ½ tsp (2 mL) cinnamon
- ¼ tsp (1 mL) salt
- 2 cups (500 mL) milk
- 1 ripe pear, coarsely grated (don't peel it)
- 2 large eggs
- 2 Tbsp (30 mL) canola oil, plus extra for cooking

A good basic pancake can be made with any number of flours; you should be fine using any combination of all-purpose, whole wheat, oat, barley, or other whole grain flours. The grated pear adds moisture and sweetness.

In a large bowl, whisk together the flour, baking powder, cinnamon, and salt. Add the milk, pear, eggs, and oil and whisk just until combined.

Set a heavy skillet over medium-high heat, drizzle it with oil, and wipe it around the pan with a paper towel. Reduce the heat to medium-low, pour in about ⅓ cup (85 mL) of the batter at a time, and cook until bubbles start to break through and the surface looks dry. Flip with a thin spatula and cook until golden on the other side.

Keep the finished pancakes warm in a 250°F (120°C) oven while you cook the rest. Serve warm topped with syrup or more sautéed pears.

SERVES 4–6

apple or pear fritter pancakes

1 cup (250 mL) all-purpose flour
1 Tbsp (15 mL) sugar
½ tsp (2 mL) cinnamon
1 tsp (5 mL) baking powder
¼ tsp (1 mL) salt
1 cup (250 mL) milk
1 large egg
1 Tbsp (15 mL) canola oil
2 tart apples or ripe but firm pears

In these pancakes, a slice of apple or pear is first sautéed to caramelize it a bit, then the batter is poured overtop. Alternatively, you can nestle a slice of fruit into the batter as it cooks in the pan, or dip the fruit in the batter before placing it in the pan.

In a large bowl, stir together the flour, sugar, cinnamon, baking powder, and salt.

In a smaller bowl, whisk together the milk, egg, and oil; add to the dry ingredients and whisk just until combined.

Cut the apples (or pears) crosswise into ¼-inch- (6 mm) thick slices; remove the middle core with the tip of a sharp knife if necessary.

Set a large, heavy skillet over medium-high heat and drizzle it with oil; swirl the oil to coat the pan. Turn the heat down to medium-low and place one or two apple or pear rings into the pan and cook for a minute or two, until golden on the bottom.

Flip, then ladle some batter overtop, letting it run into the middle and around the sides. (Alternatively, dip the fruit slices into the batter and place in the hot pan.) Cook, turning with a thin spatula, until golden on both sides. Repeat with the remaining fruit rings and batter.

If you need to keep the finished pancakes warm, keep them uncovered on a plate in a 250°F (120°C) oven. Serve warm with butter and maple syrup.

MAKES ABOUT 1 DOZEN SMALL PANCAKES

cherry cheese blintzes

CRÊPES:
1¼ cups (310 mL) milk
2 large eggs
1 Tbsp (15 mL) canola oil
¾ cup (185 mL) all-purpose flour
1 tsp (5 mL) sugar
Pinch salt

FILLING:
2 cups (500 mL) farmers' cheese or ricotta
½ cup (125 mL) full-fat sour cream, crème fraîche, or mascarpone
1 large egg
2 Tbsp (30 mL) sugar
½ tsp (2 mL) vanilla

CHERRY COMPOTE:
3 cups (750 mL) fresh or frozen cherries, pitted
½ cup (125 mL) sugar
½ cup (125 mL) water
1 tsp (5 mL) vanilla
2 tsp (10 mL) cornstarch (optional)

Oil and butter, for cooking

A blintz is a divine package of creamy, sweetened cheese enveloped in a crêpe and typically topped with cherry compote. Farmers' cheese is similar to ricotta and is commonly used in eastern European baking.

To make the crêpe batter, combine the milk, eggs, oil, flour, sugar, and salt in a blender and pulse until well blended and smooth. Let sit for 20–30 minutes; it should have the consistency of heavy cream.

To make the filling, stir together the farmers' cheese or ricotta; the sour cream, crème fraîche, or mascarpone; and the egg, sugar, and vanilla. To make the sauce, bring the cherries, sugar, and water to a simmer in a medium saucepan; cook until the cherries collapse. To thicken, stir the cornstarch into 1 Tbsp (15 mL) of cold water; add to the cherry mixture and bring to a boil. Cook for 4–5 minutes, then remove from heat and set aside to cool.

To make the crêpes, set a medium skillet over medium-high heat and drizzle with oil. Pour a few tablespoons of batter into the pan and quickly swirl it to coat the bottom or make an even circle. Cook until the edge starts to curl and it's golden on the bottom; it will now be easy to slide a thin spatula under the edge and flip the crêpe. Cook for another minute, until golden on the other side. Repeat with the remaining batter.

Filling a blintz is like filling a burrito: place a crêpe on your work surface and put about ¼ cup (60 mL) filling in a strip down the middle, leaving about an inch (2.5 cm) at each end. Fold one long side over to enclose the filling; fold each short end over, then flip the whole thing over to close. Fill all the crêpes and set aside (or refrigerate for up to a day).

When you're ready to cook your blintzes, heat a pat of butter in your skillet over medium-high heat. Cook a few at a time, without crowding the pan, until browned and crisp on both sides.

Serve warm topped with cherry compote.

MAKES 8–10 BLINTZES

apple & pear granola breakfast crisp

FRUIT BASE:

3–4 large apples, cored and diced or sliced
2 ripe but firm pears, cored and diced or sliced
⅓ cup (85 mL) sugar
½ tsp (2 mL) cinnamon

TOPPING:

1 cup (250 mL) old-fashioned or quick oats
½ cup (125 mL) whole wheat, oat, or barley flour
½ cup (125 mL) packed brown sugar
⅓ cup (85 mL) butter, cut into pieces
2 Tbsp (30 mL) pure maple syrup
½ tsp (2 mL) cinnamon
Pinch salt
¼ cup (60 mL) coconut
¼ cup (60 mL) chopped walnuts or pecans
¼ cup (60 mL) sliced almonds

Fruit is undeniably a breakfast food, as is granola. Together they make a warm, comforting crisp that's like an ultra-deluxe version of oatmeal, perfect for serving friends at brunch topped with a dollop of plain or vanilla yogurt. Or make a batch for yourself and eat it cold, scooped straight from the fridge, all week long.

Preheat the oven to 350°F (180°C).

Slice or chop the apples and pears into a baking dish or pie plate, sprinkle with sugar and cinnamon, and toss to coat.

In the bowl of a food processor (or in a medium mixing bowl), combine the oats, flour, brown sugar, butter, syrup, cinnamon, and salt and pulse or blend with a fork until well combined and crumbly. Add the coconut, walnuts, and almonds and pulse a few times to combine without grinding them too much.

Sprinkle the topping mixture over the fruit, squeezing a bit as you go to create larger clumps. Bake for 45 minutes to an hour, until the fruit is bubbly and the topping is golden.

Serve warm, at room temperature, or cold, with plain or vanilla yogurt.

SERVES 8

maple cornmeal waffles with caramelized peaches

WAFFLES:

1½ cups (375 mL) all-purpose flour
½ cup (125 mL) cornmeal
2 tsp (10 mL) baking powder
1 tsp (5 mL) baking soda
Pinch salt
2 large eggs
2 cups (500 mL) buttermilk
¼ cup (60 mL) canola oil
2 Tbsp (30 mL) pure maple syrup

PEACHES:

2 Tbsp (30 mL) butter
1–2 peaches, peeled (or not) and sliced
2 Tbsp (30 mL) brown sugar
⅓ cup (85 mL) pure maple syrup

Toasted pecans, for garnish

Cornmeal and maple syrup make a sweet, crunchy waffle that's a perfect vehicle for caramelized peaches. (Or apples, or plums . . .) For something different, crumble some cooked bacon into the batter before you cook the waffles.

In a large bowl, whisk together the flour, cornmeal, baking powder, baking soda, and salt. In another bowl, whisk together the eggs, buttermilk, oil, and syrup; pour over the dry ingredients. Stir just until blended.

Preheat your waffle iron and brush it with some oil or spray it with nonstick spray. Ladle in about ⅓ cup (85 mL) of batter, close the lid, and cook according to the manufacturer's directions or until the waffle is golden and crisp.

Meanwhile, set a heavy skillet over medium-high heat and add the butter. When the foam subsides, add the peaches to the pan and cook for 3–4 minutes, until softened. Add the brown sugar and syrup; cook until saucy and starting to turn golden.

Serve the waffles topped with caramelized peaches and toasted pecans.

MAKES ABOUT 6 LARGE WAFFLES

multi-grain apple waffles with cider syrup

- 2 cups (500 mL) apple cider
- 1 cup (250 mL) all-purpose flour
- ½ cup (125 mL) whole wheat flour
- ½ cup (125 mL) barley flour
- ¼ cup (60 mL) oat bran
- 2 Tbsp (30 mL) brown sugar
- 2 tsp (10 mL) baking powder
- ½ tsp (2 mL) cinnamon
- ¼ tsp (1 mL) salt
- 1½ cups (375 mL) milk
- 2 large eggs
- ¼ cup (60 mL) canola oil or melted butter
- 1 tsp (5 mL) vanilla
- 1 apple, cored and finely chopped

These soft, pillowy waffles are similar to pancakes in texture. The cider reduces to a deliciously sweet, tangy syrup; it can be done ahead of time, but the pectin content in apples may make it gel. If it does, rewarm to melt it before serving.

In a small saucepan, simmer the cider over medium-high heat until it's reduced to about a quarter and has the consistency of thin syrup. Set aside to cool.

In a medium bowl, whisk together the flours, oat bran, brown sugar, baking powder, cinnamon, and salt. In a small bowl, whisk together the milk, eggs, oil or butter, and vanilla. Add to the dry ingredients and whisk just until blended. Stir in the apple.

Preheat your waffle iron and spray it with nonstick spray or brush it with oil. Ladle in about ⅓ cup (85 mL) of batter, close the lid, and cook according to the manufacturer's directions or until golden and crisp. Serve immediately or keep warm on a rack set on a baking sheet in a 250°F (120°C) oven while you cook the rest.

Serve the waffles warm, drizzled with cider syrup.

MAKES ABOUT 4 LARGE OR 8 REGULAR WAFFLES

WELLS &

MUFFINS & QUICK BREADS

apple cinnamon muffins

- 2 cups (500 mL) all-purpose flour
- 2 tsp (10 mL) baking powder
- 2 tsp (10 mL) cinnamon
- ½ tsp (2 mL) salt
- ½ cup (125 mL) sugar
- ⅓ cup (85 mL) canola oil or melted butter
- 2 large eggs
- 1 cup (250 mL) milk
- 1 tsp (5 mL) vanilla
- 1 large apple, coarsely grated

In the fall, everyone should have a moist, cinnamon-spiked apple muffin in their repertoire. Add a handful of raisins or chopped nuts, if you like.

Preheat the oven to 375°F (190°C).

In a medium bowl, stir together the flour, baking powder, cinnamon, and salt.

In another bowl, whisk together the sugar, oil or melted butter, and eggs until thick and pale; whisk in the milk and vanilla. Add to the dry ingredients along with the grated apple and stir just until combined.

Divide the batter between 12 greased or paper-lined muffin cups. Bake for 25 minutes or until pale golden and springy to the touch. Tip the muffins in the pan to help them cool.

MAKES 1 DOZEN MUFFINS

crunchy pear muffins

- 2 cups (500 mL) all-purpose flour
- ½ cup (125 mL) sugar
- 1 tsp (5 mL) cinnamon
- ½ tsp (2 mL) ground ginger (optional)
- 2 tsp (10 mL) baking powder
- ¼ tsp (1 mL) salt
- 2 very ripe pears, coarsely grated (don't bother peeling them)
- 2 large eggs
- ⅓ cup (85 mL) canola or other vegetable oil
- 1 tsp (5 mL) vanilla
- 1 cup (250 mL) fresh or frozen cranberries or halved, pitted cherries (optional)
- ½ cup (125 mL) chopped walnuts or pecans (optional)

Most people set aside overripe bananas for baking; the same can be done with pears. They make a slightly sweet, aromatic, crunchy-topped muffin that can be studded with cherries, cranberries, chopped nuts, chocolate chunks—you name it.

Preheat the oven to 375°F (190°C).

In a medium bowl, stir together the flour, sugar, cinnamon, ginger, baking powder, and salt. In a smaller bowl, stir together the grated pears, eggs, oil, and vanilla. Add all at once to the dry ingredients and stir until almost combined. If you like, add some cranberries or cherries, or some chopped walnuts or pecans, and stir just until blended.

Divide the batter between 12 greased or paper-lined muffin cups and bake for 20–25 minutes or until golden and springy to the touch. Tip the muffins in the pan to help them cool.

MAKES 1 DOZEN MUFFINS

fresh peach bran muffins

- 2 cups (500 mL) 100% bran cereal
- 1¾ cups (435 mL) buttermilk, or plain yogurt thinned with milk
- ½ cup (125 mL) packed brown sugar
- ¼ cup (60 mL) canola oil
- 1 large egg
- 1½ cups (375 mL) all-purpose flour
- 2 tsp (10 mL) baking powder
- 1 tsp (5 mL) baking soda
- ¼ tsp (1 mL) salt
- 1 peach, pitted and chopped

Hearty, grainy bran muffins pair well with chopped peaches—or substitute nectarines or apricots.

In a large bowl, stir together the cereal and buttermilk or yogurt; let stand for 10 minutes, until soft. Preheat the oven to 375°F (190°C).

Stir the brown sugar, oil, and egg into the bran mixture. Add the flour, baking powder, baking soda, and salt; stir until almost combined. Add the peach and stir just until blended.

Divide the batter among 12 greased or paper-lined muffin cups. Bake for 25 minutes or until golden and springy to the touch. Tip the muffins in the pan to help them cool.

MAKES 1 DOZEN MUFFINS

morning glory muffins

- 1 cup (250 mL) all-purpose flour
- 1 cup (250 mL) whole wheat flour
- 1 cup (250 mL) sugar
- 2 tsp (10 mL) cinnamon
- 2 tsp (10 mL) baking soda
- ¼ tsp (1 mL) salt
- 2 cups (500 mL) grated carrots
- ½ cup (125 mL) chopped pecans or walnuts
- ½ cup (125 mL) raisins
- ¼ cup (60 mL) shredded coconut, sweetened or unsweetened
- ½ cup (125 mL) canola oil
- 2 large eggs
- ½ cup (125 mL) buttermilk, or plain yogurt thinned with milk
- 2 tsp (10 mL) vanilla
- 1 pear or apple, coarsely grated (don't bother peeling it)

Morning Glory Muffins are full of good things: grated carrots, apples or pears, raisins, nuts, and coconut. They make good use of an overripe pear or an apple that might have a few bruises.

Preheat the oven to 375°F (190°C).

In a large bowl, stir together the flours, sugar, cinnamon, baking soda, and salt. Add the carrots, pecans or walnuts, raisins, and coconut and toss to combine well.

In a medium bowl, whisk together the oil, eggs, buttermilk or yogurt, and vanilla. Add to the carrot mixture along with the grated pear or apple and stir just until the batter is combined. (Don't worry about getting all the lumps out.)

Divide the batter between 12 greased or paper-lined muffin cups. Bake for 25–30 minutes or until the muffins are golden and the tops are springy to the touch. Tip the muffins in the pan to help them cool.

MAKES 1 DOZEN MUFFINS

peach & pumpkin muffins

- 14 oz (398 mL) can pumpkin purée
- 1 cup (250 mL) sugar
- 1 cup (250 mL) canola oil
- 1 large egg
- 2 tsp (10 mL) vanilla
- 3 cups (750 mL) all-purpose flour
- 1 Tbsp (15 mL) cinnamon or pumpkin pie spice
- 2 tsp (10 mL) baking powder
- 1 tsp (5 mL) baking soda
- ½ tsp (2 mL) salt
- 1 large peach, pitted and finely chopped
- Coarse sugar, for sprinkling (optional)

In late summer, when the last of the peaches make way for the first pumpkins, the two make a perfect pairing in this moist, fragrant muffin.

Preheat the oven to 350°F (180°C).

In a large bowl, combine the pumpkin, sugar, oil, egg, and vanilla. In another bowl, stir together the dry ingredients (flour through salt); add to the pumpkin mixture and stir until almost combined. Add the peaches and stir just until blended.

Divide the batter among 18 greased or paper-lined muffin cups, filling them almost to the top, and sprinkle with coarse sugar if you like. Bake for 25–30 minutes or until golden and springy to the touch. Tip the muffins in the pans to help them cool.

MAKES 1½ DOZEN MUFFINS

oatmeal plum muffins

- 1½ cups (375 mL) old-fashioned or quick oats
- 1 cup (250 mL) buttermilk
- ½ cup (125 mL) milk
- 1 large egg
- ½ cup (125 mL) firmly packed light brown sugar
- ⅓ cup (85 mL) butter, melted and cooled
- 2 Tbsp (30 mL) canola oil
- 1½ cups (375 mL) all-purpose flour (or half all-purpose, half whole wheat)
- 2 tsp (10 mL) baking powder
- ½ tsp (2 mL) baking soda
- ¼ tsp (1 mL) salt
- 1 cup (250 mL) chopped plums

This is a great basic oatmeal muffin formula that can be used as a vehicle for any fruit in season; chopped fresh plums are wonderful, but so are chopped apricots, peaches, apples, and pears. Add a shake of cinnamon, if you like.

In a large bowl, combine the oats, buttermilk, and milk and let stand 1 hour. When you're ready to bake, preheat the oven to 375°F (190°C).

Add the egg, sugar, butter, and oil to the oat mixture, stirring until just combined.

In a small bowl, stir together the flour, baking powder, baking soda, and salt. Add to the wet ingredients and stir until almost combined; add the plums and stir just until blended.

Divide the batter between 12 greased or paper-lined muffin cups. Bake for 20–25 minutes or until golden and springy to the touch. Tip the muffins in the pan to help them cool.

MAKES 1 DOZEN MUFFINS

apple pie biscuits

BISCUITS:
- 1½ cups (375 mL) all-purpose flour
- 2 Tbsp (30 mL) sugar
- 1½ tsp (7 mL) baking powder
- ¼ tsp (1 mL) salt
- 1 cup (250 mL) heavy (whipping) cream

FILLING:
- 2 Tbsp (30 mL) butter
- 1 large apple, cored and thinly sliced (don't bother peeling it)
- 2 Tbsp (30 mL) sugar or brown sugar
- 1 Tbsp (15 mL) pure maple syrup, golden syrup, or honey
- ½ tsp (2 mL) cinnamon

- Extra cream or milk, for brushing (optional)
- Regular or coarse sugar, for sprinkling (optional)

Rustic filled apple biscuits were the darlings of the Internet last year courtesy of a recipe by King Arthur Flour. This version uses a super-simple cream biscuit formula to sandwich caramelized apples. Feel free to swap pears or peaches for the apples; just sauté them first to cook them down and get rid of excess juice to prevent the biscuits from getting soggy.

Preheat the oven to 400°F (200°C).

In a medium bowl, stir together the flour, sugar, baking powder, and salt. Add the cream and stir just until the dough comes together. On a piece of parchment (or a lightly floured surface), roll the dough out into a 9- × 11-inch (23 × 28 cm) rectangle.

Meanwhile, heat the butter in a small skillet over medium-high heat. When the foam subsides, add the apples and sauté for 3–4 minutes, until soft and browning on the edges. Add the sugar, syrup or honey, and cinnamon and cook for another minute, until the mixture bubbles and thickens slightly. Remove from heat.

Spread the apple mixture—with any syrup that has accumulated in the bottom of the pan—lengthwise down half of the biscuit dough and fold it over to cover. Pinch the edges to seal a bit, but don't worry about sealing the apples in completely.

Transfer to a baking sheet and cut lengthwise in half, then crosswise into eight biscuits. Pull them apart on the pan to give them room to bake. If you like, brush the tops with a little extra cream or milk and/or sprinkle with sugar.

Bake for 15–20 minutes or until golden. Serve warm.

MAKES 8 BISCUITS

vanilla pear scones

SCONES:
- 2 cups (500 mL) all-purpose flour
- ⅓ cup (85 mL) sugar
- 2 tsp (10 mL) baking powder
- ½ tsp (2 mL) baking soda
- ¼ tsp (1 mL) salt
- ½ cup (125 mL) butter, cut into chunks
- ¾ cup (185 mL) buttermilk or half & half cream
- 1 large egg
- 1 tsp (5 mL) vanilla or vanilla bean paste, or the seeds scraped from 1 vanilla bean
- 1 ripe but firm pear, cored and finely chopped
- Extra milk or cream, for brushing (optional)
- Coarse sugar, for sprinkling (optional)

VANILLA GLAZE:
- 1 cup (250 mL) icing sugar
- 1 Tbsp (15 mL) milk or cream (any kind)
- ½ tsp (2 mL) vanilla or vanilla bean paste, or the seeds scraped from 1 vanilla bean

Vanilla and pears are magical together in a warm scone. If you use vanilla bean paste—or even real vanilla beans—you'll be able to see the little vanilla seeds in the scones as well as the drizzle.

Preheat the oven to 400°F (200°C).

In a large bowl, stir together the flour, sugar, baking powder, baking soda, and salt. Add the butter and blend it with a fork, whisk, pastry blender, or your fingers (or pulse in the bowl of a food processor), leaving some lumps no bigger than a pea.

In a small bowl, stir the buttermilk, egg, and vanilla together with a fork. Add to the flour mixture and stir until almost combined. Add the pears and stir just until the dough comes together.

Pat the dough out about 1 inch (2.5 cm) thick on a parchment-lined baking sheet and cut into 8 rounds or wedges. If you like, brush with milk or cream and/or sprinkle with sugar. Pull them apart, leaving at least an inch between them. Bake for 20 minutes or until golden.

To make the glaze, whisk together the icing sugar, milk or cream, and vanilla. Drizzle it over the scones with a fork while they're still warm.

MAKES 8 SCONES

chunky peach sour cream cobbler scones

- 2 cups (500 mL) all-purpose flour
- ¼ cup (60 mL) packed brown sugar
- 2 tsp (10 mL) baking powder
- ½ tsp (2 mL) cinnamon
- ¼ tsp (1 mL) salt
- ⅓ cup (85 mL) butter, cut into pieces
- ¾ cup (185 mL) sour cream
- ¼ cup (60 mL) milk or water
- 2 tsp (10 mL) grated fresh ginger
- 1 peach, pitted and diced (don't bother peeling it)
- Coarse sugar, for sprinkling (optional)

If you like, substitute 1 tsp (5 mL) ground ginger for the fresh; it adds a more peppery flavour. These scones are also delicious with apricots or plums.

Preheat the oven to 425°F (220°C).

In a medium bowl, stir together the flour, brown sugar, baking powder, cinnamon, and salt. Add the butter and blend with a fork or your fingers until well combined and crumbly.

In a small bowl, stir together the sour cream, milk or water, and ginger. Add the chopped peaches to the flour mixture and toss to coat, then add the sour cream mixture and stir just until you have a sticky dough.

On a parchment-lined baking sheet, pat the dough into a 1-inch (2.5 cm) circle and cut into 8 wedges with a knife. (If it's too sticky, drop by the large spoonful onto the sheet.) Pull the wedges apart, leaving an inch or two between them so they bake evenly. If you like, sprinkle the tops with coarse sugar.

Bake for 15–20 minutes or until golden. Serve warm.

MAKES 8 SCONES

dark chocolate cherry scones

- 2 cups (500 mL) all-purpose flour
- ½ cup (125 mL) sugar
- ½ cup (125 mL) cocoa
- 2 tsp (10 mL) baking powder
- ¼ tsp (1 mL) salt
- ½ cup (125 mL) butter, cut into pieces
- ¾ cup (185 mL) milk or half & half cream
- 1 large egg
- 1 cup (250 mL) fresh or frozen cherries, pitted and halved
- ½ cup (125 mL) chopped dark or white chocolate
- Extra milk or cream, for brushing (optional)
- Coarse sugar, for sprinkling (optional)

With a flavour reminiscent of Black Forest cake, these decadent scones make a perfect afternoon snack.

Preheat the oven to 400°F (200°C).

In a large bowl, whisk together the flour, sugar, cocoa, baking powder, and salt. Add the butter and blend with a fork or pastry cutter (or pulse the dry ingredients and the butter in the bowl of a food processor) until almost blended, with pieces of butter no bigger than a pea.

In a small bowl or measuring cup, stir together the milk or cream and the egg with a fork. Add to the dry ingredients and stir a few strokes, then add the cherries and chocolate and stir just until the dough comes together.

On a parchment-lined baking sheet, pat the dough out 1 inch (2.5 cm) thick and cut out 8–12 rounds or wedges. Pull them apart so they have at least an inch between them. If you like, brush the tops with milk or cream and/or sprinkle with sugar.

Bake for 20 minutes or until deep golden and set. Serve warm.

MAKES 8–12 SCONES

cinnamon apple raisin irish soda bread

- 3½ cups (875 mL) all-purpose flour
- ½ cup (125 mL) old-fashioned oats
- ¼ cup (60 mL) sugar
- 2 tsp (10 mL) cinnamon
- 2 tsp (10 mL) baking soda
- ½ tsp (2 mL) salt
- ¼ cup (60 mL) butter, cut into pieces
- ½–1 cup (125–250 mL) raisins
- 1½ cups (375 mL) buttermilk, or plain yogurt, thinned with milk
- 1 large egg
- 1 large apple, coarsely grated (don't bother peeling it)

A rustic loaf of Irish soda bread is an invaluable thing to know how to make. It's substantial compared to other quick loaves and is served in wedges for a comforting breakfast or alongside a cup of tea. Apples add sweetness and flavour; pears could be substituted, or add a half cup of chopped walnuts or pecans along with the raisins.

Preheat the oven to 375°F (190°C).

In a large bowl, stir together the flour, oats, sugar, cinnamon, baking soda, and salt. Add the butter and blend with a fork or your fingers until crumbly. Add the raisins and toss to combine.

In a mixing bowl or measuring cup, stir together the buttermilk or yogurt and the egg with a fork, and add all at once to the dry ingredients, along with the grated apple. Stir just until combined, then scrape onto a buttered or parchment-lined baking sheet and, with dampened hands, shape into a rough domed circle.

Cut an X into the top and bake for an hour or until golden and the bottom sounds hollow when tapped. Cool slightly before cutting into wedges.

MAKES 1 LOAF

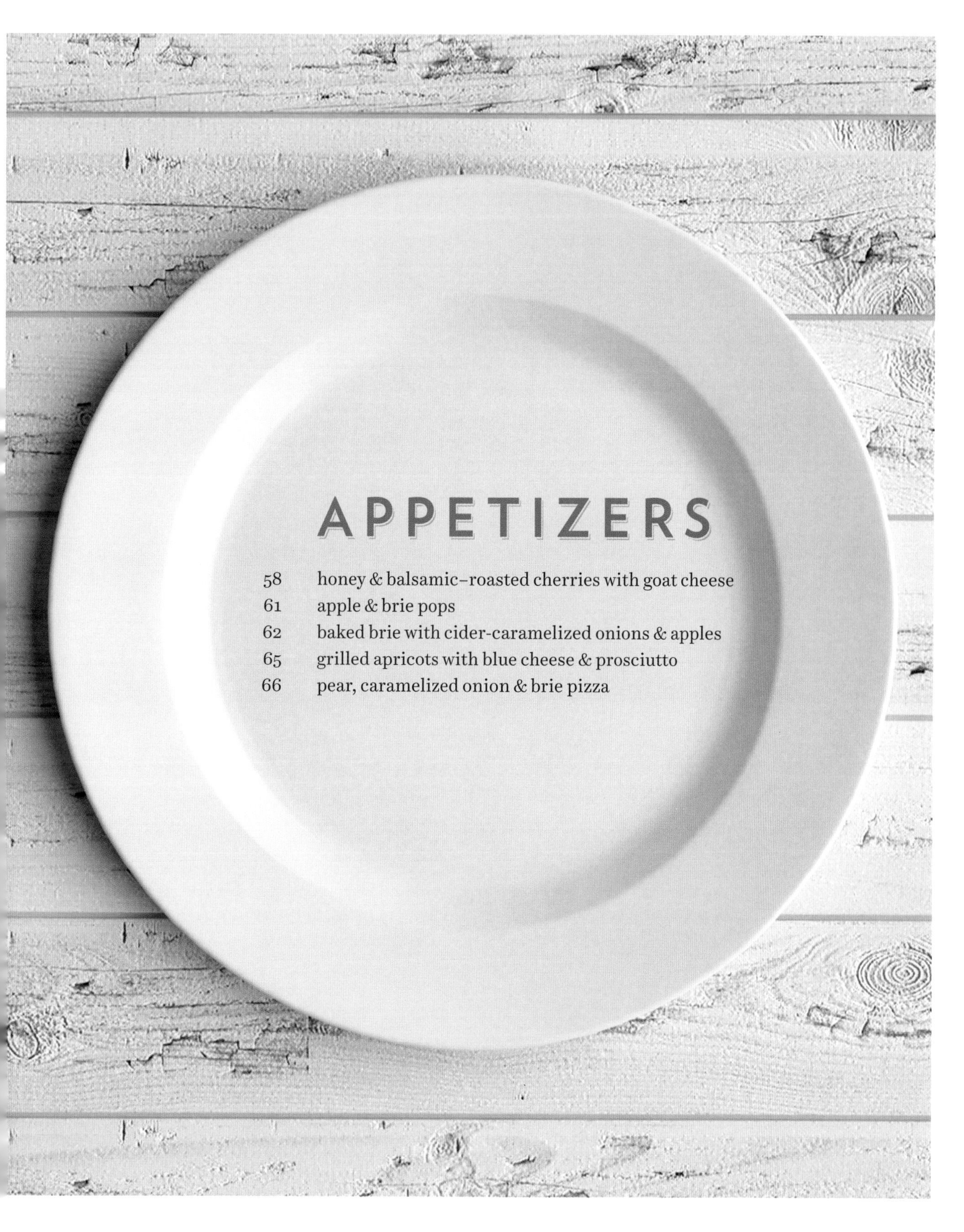

APPETIZERS

honey & balsamic–roasted cherries with goat cheese

Fresh cherries, pitted
Honey
Balsamic vinegar
Extra-virgin olive oil
Sprig of fresh rosemary (optional)
Freshly ground black pepper (optional)
1 log soft goat cheese
1 crusty baguette or crackers

When cherries are in season, this is the ultimate patio snack. Roast as many cherries as you like and serve them over a log of soft goat cheese with a crusty baguette.

Preheat the oven to 400°F (200°C).

Spread the cherries out in a single layer on a parchment-lined rimmed baking sheet. Whisk together equal amounts of honey and balsamic vinegar with about half as much oil (about ¼ cup/60 mL honey and balsamic and 2 Tbsp/30 mL oil for 4 cups/1 L cherries) and pour over the cherries. If you like, add a sprig of rosemary and toss to coat, and/or grind over a bit of black pepper.

Roast for 10–20 minutes, stirring once or twice, until the cherries soften and release their juices and everything gets dark and sticky. Serve warm with the goat cheese and slices of crusty baguette for spreading.

SERVES AS MANY AS YOU LIKE

SAUVIGNON

apple & brie pops

2 Tbsp (30 mL) butter
1 tart apple, cored and finely chopped
1 tsp (5 mL) chopped fresh rosemary
1 Tbsp (15 mL) honey
1 package puff pastry, thawed but cold
4 oz (125 g) Brie, sliced
1 egg, lightly beaten

Apples and Brie stuffed inside puff pastry and served on a stick is the ultimate party food. If you like, omit the stick to make little square tarts that are perfect for nibbling with wine.

Preheat the oven to 400°F (200°C).

Put the butter in a small skillet set over medium-high heat and sauté the apple and rosemary for 3–4 minutes, until soft and starting to turn golden. Add the honey and stir until caramelized. Remove from heat and transfer to a bowl to cool.

On a lightly floured surface, unroll (or roll out) each piece of thawed puff pastry into about an 8- × 10-inch (20 × 25 cm) rectangle, and cut each into 12 rectangles. Top half of the rectangles with a small piece of Brie and a spoonful of sautéed apple.

Brush the edges with beaten egg and, if you like, place a wooden Popsicle stick or coffee stir stick on one short side so that the stick overlaps the pastry by about ½ inch (1 cm). Top with the remaining pastry rectangles and press the edges with the tines of a fork to seal. Place on a parchment-lined baking sheet, brush the tops with more egg wash, and poke with a fork to help steam escape.

Bake for 15–20 minutes or until golden.

MAKES 1 DOZEN POPS

baked brie with cider-caramelized onions & apples

Olive or canola oil, for cooking
2 Tbsp (30 mL) butter
1 large sweet onion, halved and thinly sliced
1 Tbsp (15 mL) balsamic vinegar (optional)
½ cup (125 mL) apple cider
1 tart apple or ripe but firm pear, cored and thinly sliced
1 Tbsp (15 mL) chopped fresh rosemary
1 small or ¼ medium wheel of Brie

Who doesn't love a gooey baked Brie? Apples (or pears) caramelized with onions and some fresh rosemary make it about as good as it gets.

Preheat the oven to 350°F (180°C).

Set a medium skillet over medium-high heat and add a drizzle of oil along with the butter. When the foam subsides, add the onion and cook for 7–8 minutes, until golden.

Add the balsamic vinegar and cook until the excess liquid cooks off. Add the cider, chopped apple or pear, and rosemary and cook until the apples soften and the mixture thickens. (This will be faster with pears.)

Place the Brie in a baking dish or on a parchment-lined baking sheet and, if you like, slice off the top rind, then top with the apple-onion mixture. Bake for 8–10 minutes or until the Brie starts to ooze. Serve immediately with crackers or crusty bread.

SERVES 6

grilled apricots with blue cheese & prosciutto

- ½ cup (125 mL) blue cheese (about 4 oz/125 g), cut into pieces
- 8 fresh apricots, halved lengthwise and pitted
- 8 thin slices prosciutto, halved lengthwise
- Extra-virgin olive oil
- Salt and freshly ground black pepper

Fresh apricots bundled up with blue cheese and bound with prosciutto are delicious uncooked, but a quick turn on the grill crisps up the prosciutto, melts the cheese a little, and softens the apricots just enough that they start releasing their juices. It's the perfect backyard appy.

Place a small piece of blue cheese in each apricot half, then wrap each in a piece of prosciutto, covering the cheese.

Brush with olive oil and sprinkle with salt and pepper. Preheat the grill to high (or turn on the oven to 450°F/230°C) and grill or roast for a few minutes, until the edges start to turn golden and the apricots soften. Serve warm.

MAKES 16 APPETIZERS

pear, caramelized onion & brie pizza

PIZZA DOUGH:

1 package (or 2 tsp/ 10 mL) active dry yeast
1 tsp (5 mL) sugar or honey
2½–3 cups (625–750 mL) all-purpose flour
2 Tbsp (30 mL) extra-virgin olive oil
1 tsp (5 mL) salt

TOPPING:

Canola oil, for cooking
2 large onions, halved and thinly sliced
1 pear, thinly sliced
4 oz (125 g) Brie or Camembert cheese, sliced
1 Tbsp (15 mL) chopped fresh rosemary
Salt and freshly ground black pepper
Olive oil, for drizzling

Thinly sliced pears, caramelized onions, and creamy Brie make for an elegant pizza. Served in thin slices, this is perfect for a cocktail party.

Put 1 cup (250 mL) warm water into a large bowl and sprinkle the yeast and sugar or honey overtop; let stand for 5 minutes, until it gets foamy. (If it doesn't, toss it out and buy fresh yeast!)

Add 2½ cups (625 mL) flour and the olive oil and salt; stir until you have a shaggy dough. Let rest for 20 minutes, then knead until smooth and elastic, adding more flour if you need it; the dough should be tacky but not too sticky.

Place the dough in an oiled bowl and turn to coat all over. Cover with a tea towel and set aside in a warm place for about an hour, until doubled in bulk. (Alternatively, let it rise more slowly in the refrigerator for up to 8 hours.)

Meanwhile, heat a generous drizzle of oil in a medium skillet set over medium-high heat and sauté the onions for 5 minutes, until soft and turning golden. Preheat the oven to 450°F (230°C).

Divide the dough in half and roll or stretch each out into a 9-inch (23 cm) circle or oval. Place each on a parchment-lined or floured baking sheet and top with half the caramelized onions, half the pear slices, and half the Brie or Camembert. Sprinkle each with rosemary, salt, and pepper and drizzle with olive oil.

Bake for 15–20 minutes, until deep golden. Let rest for a few minutes before slicing.

MAKES 2 PIZZAS; SERVES 12–16

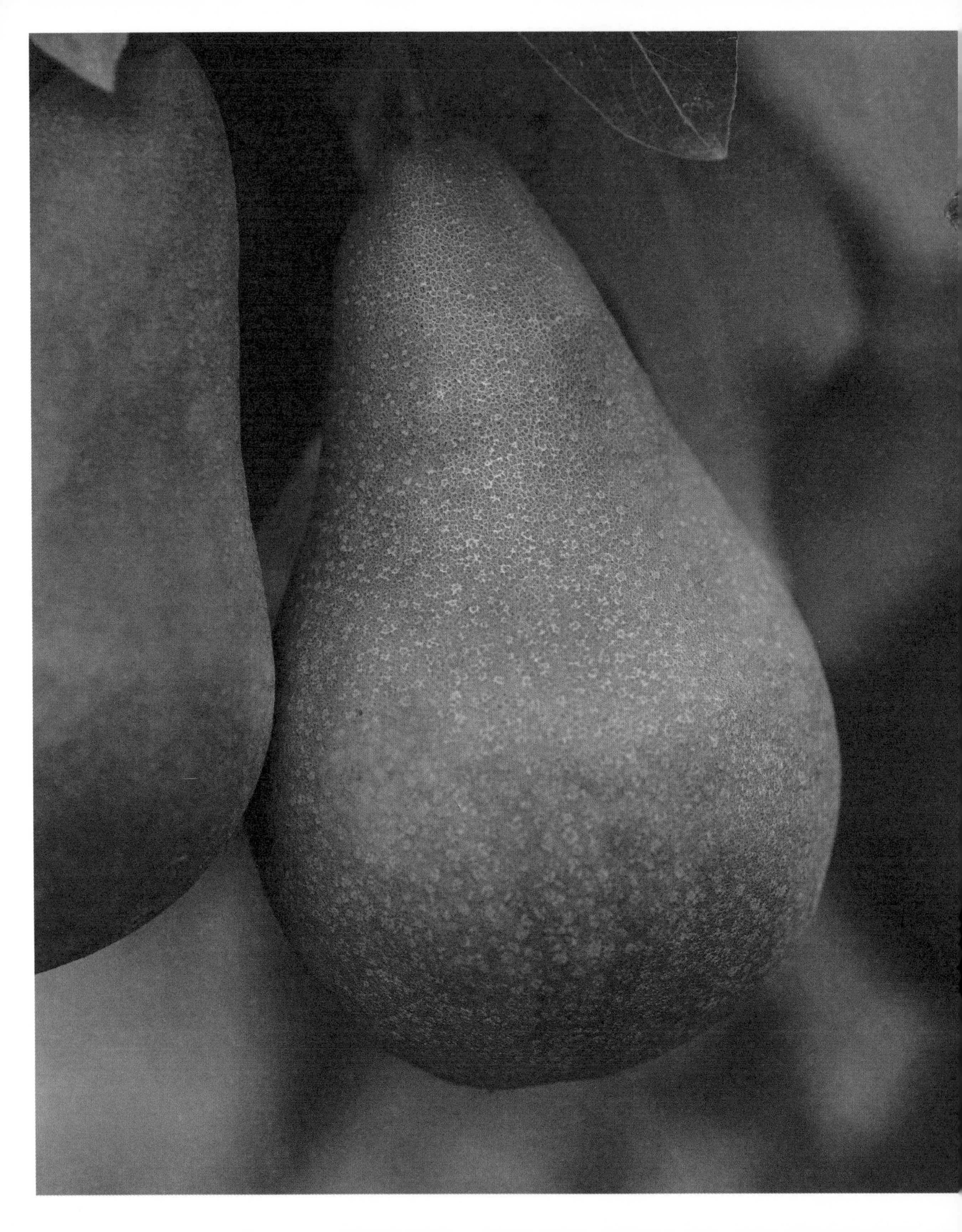

SOUPS, SALADS & SIDES

roasted carrot soup with apples and sage

2 lb (1 kg) carrots, peeled (or scrubbed) and cut into 1-inch (2.5 cm) chunks
Canola oil, for cooking
1 Tbsp (15 mL) butter
1 onion, peeled and chopped
1 tart apple, cored and chopped
1–2 Tbsp (15–30 mL) chopped fresh sage
3–4 cups (750 mL–1 L) chicken stock
1 cup (250 mL) apple cider
Salt and freshly ground black pepper, to taste
½ cup (125 mL) half & half or heavy (whipping) cream (optional)

Next time you roast carrots for dinner, throw in a few extra; they make a delicious soup spiked with sage and sweetened with apples and cider.

Preheat the oven to 450°F (230°C).

Spread the carrots out in a single layer on a rimmed baking sheet and drizzle with oil; toss to coat well. Roast for 20 minutes or until soft and starting to turn golden on the edges.

In a medium pot, heat a drizzle of oil with the butter over medium-high heat. When the foam subsides, add the onion and cook for 4–5 minutes, until soft. Add the apple, sage, roasted carrots (scraping any flavourful browned bits from the pan), stock, and cider and bring to a simmer. Cook for 15–20 minutes or until everything is nice and soft. Season with salt and pepper.

Remove from heat and, using a hand-held immersion blender, purée the soup right in the pot. (Alternatively, process it in a blender in batches until smooth.) Stir in the cream, if you're using it. Serve hot.

SERVES 6

curried sweet potato, carrot & red lentil soup with ginger & pear

Canola oil, for cooking
1 onion, chopped
2 garlic cloves, crushed
1 Tbsp (15 mL) grated fresh ginger
½ cup (125 mL) dry red lentils
1 medium dark-fleshed sweet potato, peeled and cut into chunks
2 carrots, peeled and chopped
1 ripe pear, cored and chopped
2 tsp (10 mL) curry paste or powder, or to taste
4 cups (1 L) chicken or vegetable stock
Salt, to taste
½ cup (125 mL) half & half or heavy (whipping) cream, or coconut milk

This delicious, smooth soup gets a boost of fibre and protein from red lentils, which go in dry and simmer along with the other ingredients. It can be made vegan with vegetable stock and coconut milk.

In a medium pot, heat a drizzle of oil over medium-high heat and sauté the onion, garlic, and ginger for 4–5 minutes, until soft. Add the lentils, sweet potato, carrots, pear, curry paste or powder, and stock, along with 2 cups (500 mL) of water. Bring to a boil, then turn the heat down and simmer for ½ hour, until the vegetables are very tender.

Season with salt, then add the cream or coconut milk (if you're using it). Use a hand-held immersion blender to purée the soup right in the pot. Alternatively, transfer the soup in batches to a blender and purée until smooth, or mash it roughly with a potato masher.

SERVES 6

pear & parsnip soup

Canola oil, for cooking
1 onion, peeled and chopped
2 garlic cloves, crushed
3 large parsnips, peeled and chopped
1 large ripe pear, cored and chopped
2 tsp (10 mL) fresh thyme
4 cups (1 L) chicken stock
1 cup (250 mL) heavy (whipping) cream
Salt and freshly ground black pepper

Earthy, nutty parsnips resemble wide, white carrots. They're in season in the fall and can be stored, like other root veggies, throughout the winter. They make a fabulous soup sweetened with ripe pear.

In a large saucepan or small pot, heat a drizzle of oil over medium-high heat and sauté the onion for 4–5 minutes, until soft. Add the garlic and cook for another minute.

Add the parsnips, pear, thyme, and stock along with 2 cups (500 mL) of water and bring to a simmer. Cook for 20–30 minutes, until the parsnips are very soft.

Add the cream, season with salt and pepper, and purée the soup right in the pot with a hand-held immersion blender, or carefully transfer it in batches to a blender to purée until smooth.

SERVES 4–6

maple-roasted butternut squash soup with apples

1 medium butternut squash
Canola or olive oil, for drizzling and cooking
2 Tbsp (30 mL) pure maple syrup
Salt and freshly ground black pepper, to taste
2 Tbsp (30 mL) butter
1 onion, chopped
1 tart apple, peeled, cored, and chopped
½–1 tsp (2–5 mL) sage or curry powder
4 cups (1 L) chicken or veggie stock
1 cup (250 mL) apple cider (optional)
½–1 cup (125–250 mL) half & half cream, 18% coffee cream, or heavy (whipping) cream

Winter squash and apples are a classic pairing. Butternut squash is among the most common and easiest to peel, but feel free to swap acorn, hubbard, or whatever type of winter squash you come across at the market. Roasting squash halves makes it easier to scoop out the flesh.

Preheat the oven to 425°F (220°C).

Cut the squash in half lengthwise, scoop out the seeds, drizzle with oil and syrup, and sprinkle with salt and pepper. Roast for 25–30 minutes or until golden. (It doesn't matter if the pieces aren't fully cooked through yet; you just want to get a bit of colour on them.)

In a small pot, heat another drizzle of oil and the butter over medium-high heat. When the foam subsides, add the onion and sauté for 3–4 minutes, until soft. Scoop the softened squash into the pot (or peel it and cut it into cubes), add the apple and the sage or curry powder, and cook for another minute. Add the stock and cider (if using) and bring to a simmer; cook for 20–30 minutes, until the squash is soft.

Add the cream, season with salt and pepper, and purée with a hand-held immersion blender. (Alternatively, purée the soup in a regular blender or mash it in the pot with a potato masher until chunky.) Add a little water, cream, or stock if it seems too thick.

SERVES 6

quinoa salad with chickpeas, feta & apples

SALAD:

1 cup (250 mL) quinoa
¼ cup (60 mL) golden or sultana raisins
19 oz (540 mL) can chickpeas, rinsed and drained
Big handful of flat-leaf parsley, chopped
½ cup (125 mL) crumbled feta (or as much as you want)
1 tart apple or ripe but firm pear, cored and chopped
½ cup (125 mL) chopped walnuts or sliced almonds, toasted

DRESSING:

¼ cup (60 mL) canola or olive oil
2 Tbsp (30 mL) rice vinegar or lemon juice
1 tsp (5 mL) honey
¼ tsp (1 mL) curry paste or powder

This is one of my favourite salads. Because it's so portable, it's perfect for bringing to parties or potlucks or even for lunch at work.

Cook the quinoa according to package directions (or in plenty of water for about 12 minutes, until tender and there's no longer a white dot in the middle). Drain well in a sieve and transfer to a wide salad bowl, add the raisins, and set aside to cool.

Once the quinoa has cooled, add the chickpeas, parsley, feta, and apple.

To make the dressing, shake all the ingredients in a jar or whisk them together in a bowl. Drizzle over the salad and toss to coat. Sprinkle with toasted walnuts or almonds right before serving.

SERVES 4–6

asian kale & pear slaw

DRESSING:

¼ cup (60 mL) canola or olive oil
¼ cup (60 mL) rice vinegar
3 Tbsp (45 mL) soy sauce
2 Tbsp (30 mL) brown sugar
1 tsp (5 mL) grated fresh ginger
1 garlic clove, finely crushed
1 tsp (5 mL) sesame oil

SLAW:

1 bunch kale, thinly sliced (discard stems)
2 ripe but firm pears (even green is okay) or tart apples, cored and thinly julienned
1–2 carrots, coarsely grated
½ red pepper, thinly sliced
4–6 pea pods, sliced or chopped
2 green onions, chopped
⅓ cup (85 mL) chopped fresh cilantro (optional)
⅓ cup (85 mL) chopped salted peanuts or sunflower seeds

Kale paired with an Asian dressing makes for a different kind of slaw. The julienned pear adds sweetness and crunch, and apples would work just as well. Feel free to experiment with other veggies: carrots, peppers, pea shoots, and even coarsely shredded broccoli stems are delicious.

To make the dressing, shake all the ingredients in a jar.

Thinly slice all the veggies into a bowl, drizzle with dressing, and toss to coat well. If you like, let the mixture sit for a bit to marinate; this will help tame the kale.

Sprinkle with peanuts or sunflower seeds right before serving.

SERVES 6

browned butter kale salad with hazelnuts & pears

- ¼ cup (60 mL) butter
- ½ bunch kale, leaves removed and thinly sliced
- 4–5 Brussels sprouts, thinly sliced or shaved and stem ends discarded (optional)
- 1–2 Tbsp (15–30 mL) lemon juice
- Salt and freshly ground black pepper, to taste
- 1 ripe but firm pear, cored and chopped
- ½ cup (125 mL) roughly chopped hazelnuts or almonds, toasted
- ¼–½ cup (60–125 mL) grated Parmesan cheese or aged Gouda

Warm browned butter helps tame the kale, wilting it just slightly, making it easier to eat. It's also a divine alternative to the usual oil-based vinaigrettes.

In a small saucepan, melt the butter over medium-high heat. Continue cooking, swirling the pan occasionally, until the foam starts turning golden and nutty-smelling. Remove from heat.

Put the kale and Brussels sprouts in a bowl; drizzle with the browned butter, scraping out the bottom of the pan to get any browned bits, and toss to coat well.

Add the lemon juice and season with salt and pepper. Add the pear, hazelnuts or almonds, and Parmesan or Gouda cheese. Toss and serve.

SERVES 4–6

braised red cabbage with cherries

- 2 Tbsp (30 mL) butter
- 1 small red cabbage, cored and thinly sliced
- 2 cups (500 mL) fresh or frozen cherries, pitted
- ¼ cup (60 mL) red wine
- 2 Tbsp (30 mL) balsamic or apple cider vinegar
- ¼ cup (60 mL) apple cider
- ¼ cup (60 mL) honey or brown sugar
- 1 cinnamon stick
- Salt and freshly ground black pepper

My Flemish grandmother used to make braised red cabbage with apple cider; cherries make a delicious addition. It's a warm, comforting, and unique side dish for those who like things sweet and tangy.

Preheat the oven to 325°F (160°C).

In a medium ovenproof pot, melt the butter over medium-high heat. When the foaming subsides, add the rest of the ingredients and cook over low heat until warmed through, then put the lid on and pop it into the oven for 1½–2 hours, until the cabbage is cooked through and the liquid thickened a bit.

Taste and add a little more honey or sugar and/or vinegar as you like to suit your taste (or apple cider if it needs a bit more liquid), and bake a little longer or simmer on the stovetop with the lid off if you want to cook it down a bit.

Serve immediately or cool and refrigerate for a day or two. The flavour will improve with some time in the fridge.

SERVES 6–8

caramelized apple-stuffed roasted sweet potatoes

- 4 small–medium dark-fleshed sweet potatoes
- 1 Tbsp (15 mL) canola oil
- 2 Tbsp (30 mL) butter
- 1 large tart apple, cored and thinly sliced, then chopped
- ¼ cup (60 mL) chopped pecans
- ¼ cup (60 mL) packed brown sugar
- ⅓ cup (85 mL) pure maple syrup
- Pinch salt

A roasted sweet potato is a glorious thing—especially when stuffed with something equally delicious, like caramelized apples and chunky pecans.

Preheat the oven to 350°F (180°C).

Poke each potato with a fork and place directly on the oven rack. Bake for 45 minutes to an hour, or until soft. Remove and set aside until cool enough to handle. (Potatoes can be baked up to this point and refrigerated for up to 3 days until you're ready for them.)

Set a medium skillet over medium-high heat and add the oil and butter. When the foaming subsides, add the apple and sauté for a few minutes, until soft. Add the pecans, brown sugar, syrup, and salt and cook until thickened.

Split each potato lengthwise and fill with the sautéed apple mixture. Return to the oven for a few minutes, until heated through.

SERVES 4

cider-baked beans with peaches

3–4 slices bacon
1 onion, finely chopped
Two 19 oz (540 mL) cans white kidney or navy beans, drained
19 oz (540 mL) can red kidney beans, drained
1 large peach, peeled, pitted, and chopped
½ cup (125 mL) ketchup
½ cup (125 mL) barbecue sauce
1 cup (250 mL) apple cider
¼ cup (60 mL) apple cider vinegar
¼ cup (60 mL) packed brown sugar
¼ cup (60 mL) grainy mustard
1 Tbsp (15 mL) molasses
Salt and freshly ground black pepper, to taste

If you want to start with dried beans, soak them overnight, then drain, cover with fresh water, and simmer until tender (about an hour) before proceeding with the recipe. Each 19 oz (540 mL) can contains about 2 cups (500 mL) of cooked beans.

In a heavy skillet, cook the bacon until crisp. Remove it from the pan, crumble, and set aside. Sauté the onion in the bacon drippings for 4–5 minutes, until soft.

Add the beans, peach, ketchup, barbecue sauce, cider, vinegar, brown sugar, mustard, molasses, and salt and pepper and bring to a simmer. Cook for 30–45 minutes, until thick. Serve warm.

SERVES 6

chana masala with apples

Canola oil, for cooking
1 Tbsp (15 mL) butter
1 small onion, finely chopped
1 jalapeño pepper, seeded and finely chopped
1 Tbsp (15 mL) grated fresh ginger
2 garlic cloves, chopped
2 tsp (10 mL) curry powder or paste
¼ cup (60 mL) chopped cilantro stems
1 large tomato, diced
One to two 19 oz (540 mL) can(s) chickpeas, drained
½ cup (125 mL) chicken stock or water
1 small tart apple, cored and diced
½ cup (125 mL) cream (heavy/whipping or half & half) or coconut milk
Salt
Extra cilantro, for serving

A can or two of chickpeas on the shelf means a quick curry isn't far away. A chopped tart apple adds a burst of sweetness that contrasts well with the spice. Like most curries, this will taste even better the next day.

Set a large, heavy skillet over medium-high heat and add a drizzle of oil along with the butter. Sauté the onion for 4–5 minutes, until soft. Add the jalapeño pepper, ginger, and garlic and cook for another minute or two. Stir in the curry powder or paste, cilantro stems, and tomato and cook for another minute.

Add the chickpeas and stock or water, bring to a simmer, and cook for about 20 minutes, until thickened. Stir in the apple and cream or coconut milk and continue to cook for 3–4 minutes. Season with salt.

Serve immediately, or cool and refrigerate overnight to allow the flavours to blend. Serve warm topped with fresh cilantro.

SERVES 4–6

MAINS

cider-roasted salmon with thyme

1 cup (250 mL) apple cider
1¾ lb (875 g) filet fresh salmon or steelhead trout
Extra-virgin olive oil
Salt and freshly ground black pepper
2–3 sprigs fresh thyme

I hadn't considered the possibility of apples with salmon until writing this book. Turns out the reduced cider is delicious over the roasted fish and takes about as much time to cook down to a syrup as it does to prep and cook the salmon.

Heat the apple cider in a small saucepan set over medium-high heat and simmer until it's reduced to about a quarter and has the consistency of runny syrup.

Meanwhile, preheat the oven to 400°F (200°C). Put the salmon or steelhead trout skin side down on a parchment-lined rimmed baking sheet. Drizzle with olive oil, sprinkle with salt and pepper, and pull the leaves off of a few sprigs of thyme to sprinkle overtop.

Roast for 15–20 minutes, until the fat rises to the surface and the fish flakes at the thin end but is still moist in the middle. Serve drizzled with the reduced cider.

SERVES 4–6

chili-rubbed fish tacos with peach & apricot salsa

FISH:

¾ lb (375 g) salmon or halibut fillet
2 tsp (10 mL) canola oil
1 tsp (5 mL) canned chipotle chilies en adobo (optional)
1 tsp (5 mL) lime juice
1 tsp (5 mL) chili powder
1 tsp (5 mL) brown sugar
½ tsp (2 mL) dried oregano
1 garlic clove, crushed
Salt and freshly ground black pepper

SALSA:

1 peach or nectarine, pitted and finely diced
1 apricot, pitted and finely diced
¼ cup (60 mL) finely chopped red onion
¼ cup (60 mL) chopped fresh cilantro
1 small jalapeño pepper, seeded and finely chopped
1 Tbsp (15 mL) lime juice
Salt

8 small flour tortillas

Fresh fish tacos are real fast food; if you don't want to bother with the assembly, the roasted fish is delicious on its own topped with fresh fruit salsa.

Place the salmon or halibut on a parchment-lined baking sheet. Combine the oil, chipotle chilies, lime juice, chili powder, brown sugar, oregano, garlic, and salt and pepper to make a paste, and rub it all over the fish. Let it stand while you preheat the oven to 425°F (220°C).

To make the salsa, toss all the ingredients together in a medium bowl, seasoning with salt to taste. Set aside.

Roast the fish for about 10 minutes per inch (2.5 cm), until the edge flakes with a fork but it's still moist in the middle. Set aside while you warm the tortillas in the microwave or wrapped in foil in the warm oven.

Flake the fish and use it to stuff the tortillas. Top with fruit salsa and serve immediately.

SERVES 4

rosemary cider-glazed baked ham with apples or pears

- 1 fully cooked bone-in or spiral-cut ham (about 6–8 lb/2.7–3.5 kg)
- 2 cups (500 mL) apple cider
- 1 sprig fresh rosemary
- 3–4 ripe but firm pears

A baked ham is perfect for serving a crowd; it's just as delicious at room temperature as it is hot, so it's great for a buffet.

Preheat the oven to 350°F (180°C) and line a roasting pan with foil.

Place the ham in the pan and bake for an hour. Meanwhile, heat the apple cider with the sprig of rosemary in a saucepan set over medium-high heat and simmer until it's reduced to about a quarter and has the consistency of runny syrup. Remove and discard the rosemary.

Cut the pears lengthwise into eighths, keeping the stems intact. Cut out the core from each wedge if necessary.

Remove the ham from the oven and baste with reduced cider; put the pear wedges around the ham, tossing them to coat in the pan drippings. (If there aren't any drippings, drizzle the pears with a bit of oil.) Return to the oven for another ½ hour to an hour, brushing once or twice with more glaze, until the exterior is sticky and golden and the ham is heated through.

Let rest for 10 minutes before carving, and serve with the roasted pears.

SERVES 10 OR MORE

maple roast pork tenderloin with apples

- 1½ cups (375 mL) apple cider, divided, or more to taste
- ⅓ cup (85 mL) pure maple syrup
- 2 Tbsp (30 mL) Dijon or grainy mustard
- 2 Tbsp (30 mL) chopped fresh rosemary
- 2 Tbsp (30 mL) lemon juice
- 2 Tbsp (30 mL) soy sauce
- 2 pork tenderloins (¾–1 lb/375–500 g each)
- Canola oil, for cooking
- 1 Tbsp (15 mL) butter
- 2 tart apples, cored and sliced
- 1 tsp (5 mL) cornstarch

This is one of our family's favourite meals: pork tenderloin marinated in maple syrup and cider, then roasted, topped with sautéed apples and the cooked-down marinade as an intensely flavoured, sweet, and tangy sauce. It needs mashed potatoes to catch any drips.

In a small bowl, whisk together ½ cup (125 mL) of the cider, the maple syrup, mustard, rosemary, lemon juice, and soy sauce. Pour over the pork and marinate for at least 2 hours, or overnight.

When you're ready to cook, preheat the oven to 400°F (200°C). Heat a drizzle of oil in a large skillet set over medium-high heat. Remove the pork, reserving the marinade, and brown the tenderloins on all sides, turning as necessary. (Don't worry about cooking them through.)

Transfer the pork to a baking dish and bake for 15–20 minutes. (If you have a meat thermometer, it should register 155°F/68°C.) Transfer the tenderloins to a cutting board, cover them with foil, and let them stand for 5–10 minutes.

Meanwhile, add the butter to the skillet (don't wash it out; you need those crispy browned bits) and sauté the apples for 5–7 minutes, until the apples are tender and golden. Add the marinade and the remaining apple cider to the pan and bring to a simmer, scraping up any flavourful browned bits stuck to the bottom of the pan.

In a small dish, stir the cornstarch into 1 Tbsp (15 mL) cold water and add to the sauce. Bring to a simmer and cook for about 5 minutes, until the sauce is slightly thickened.

Slice the pork and serve topped with the apples and sauce.

SERVES 6

pork & apple tourtière

FILLING:

Canola oil, for cooking
1 onion, finely chopped
1½ lb (750 g) ground pork
2 celery stalks, chopped (with leaves)
1 tart apple, cored and diced
2 garlic cloves, crushed
½ tsp (2 mL) sage
¼ tsp (1 mL) each cinnamon, nutmeg, and allspice
Salt and freshly ground black pepper

PASTRY:

1 package puff pastry, thawed but cold
1 egg, lightly beaten

A classic pork tourtière with sage and warm apple pie spices is a perfect vehicle for chopped apples. This version is simple, with only a puff pastry lid; make a big one for sharing or fill individual ovenproof dishes and top each with a circle of pastry.

Preheat the oven to 400°F (200°C).

Set a large, heavy skillet over medium-high heat and add a drizzle of oil. Sauté the onion for 3–4 minutes, until soft. Add the ground pork and cook, breaking up the meat until it's no longer pink.

Add the celery, apple, and garlic and cook for 3–4 more minutes, then stir in the sage, cinnamon, nutmeg, and allspice and season with salt and pepper. Transfer to a baking dish or individual baking dishes.

On a lightly floured surface, roll out the puff pastry to ¼ inch (6 mm) thick and cut into rounds slightly larger than the top of your baking dish(es). Brush around the edge of the baking dish(es) with beaten egg; this will act like glue to help the pastry adhere.

Top the baking dish(es) with the pastry, cut a few slits in the top to help steam escape, and brush the tops with egg.

Bake for 20–30 minutes, or until golden.

SERVES 4–6

pulled pork with peaches

Canola oil, for cooking
3–4 lb (1.5–1.8 kg) pork shoulder
1 onion, halved and thinly sliced
2 peaches, sliced or chopped (don't bother peeling them)
⅓ cup (85 mL) packed brown sugar
⅓ cup (85 mL) apple cider vinegar
⅓ cup (85 mL) ketchup
1 Tbsp (15 mL) Worcestershire sauce
2 garlic cloves, crushed
Barbecue sauce, to taste
Soft buns or biscuits, for serving

Ripe peaches make a perfect addition to pulled pork and barbecue sauce, adding sweetness and just the right amount of tang. This is easy to do in the slow cooker. Alternatively, add a cup (250 mL) of apple cider to the mix and braise it in the oven at 300°F (150°C) for 3 hours.

In a heavy skillet, heat a drizzle of oil over medium-high heat and brown the pork on all sides, turning it with tongs.

Transfer to a slow cooker and add the onions to the pan, stirring them around to loosen any browned bits. Add them to the slow cooker along with the peaches, brown sugar, apple cider vinegar, ketchup, Worcestershire sauce, and garlic. (If you like, add a glug of barbecue sauce too.) Cover and cook on low heat for 6–8 hours.

Pull the pork apart with two forks right in the bowl of the slow cooker, and leave the lid off for a while to reduce the sauce a bit. Add some barbecue sauce if you like as you pull the meat apart; otherwise, serve it alongside for people to add their own. Serve on soft buns or biscuits.

SERVES 8–10

crown roast of pork with rosemary stuffing & roasted apples

PORK:

- 5–6 lb (2.2–2.7 kg) crown roast of pork (about 10 bones)
- Canola or olive oil, for cooking
- Salt and freshly ground black pepper, to taste
- 4 tart apples, cored and cut into thick wedges, or ripe but firm pears, cored and quartered lengthwise
- 1 cup (250 mL) fresh or frozen cherries, pitted (optional)

STUFFING:

- ¼ cup (60 mL) canola or olive oil
- ¼ cup (60 mL) butter
- 1 onion, peeled and chopped
- 2 celery stalks, with leaves, chopped
- 1 small tart apple or pear, cored and chopped
- 1 Tbsp (15 mL) chopped fresh rosemary
- 1 small, day-old loaf of round crusty bread
- 1 cup (250 mL) chicken or vegetable stock
- Salt and freshly ground black pepper, to taste

Crown roast of pork is impressive to serve, easy to carve, and a perfect alternative to turkey when you're making a special dinner for a small crowd. And it's far easier to stuff than a turkey; simply mound the stuffing in the middle.

If the butcher hasn't already done so, separate the bones by cutting between them with a sharp knife. If you like, French the bones by carefully scraping off any bits of meat with a knife.

Place the pork in a roasting pan or large cast iron pan and drizzle with oil. Rub the oil all over the meat and sprinkle with salt and pepper. Arrange the apples or pears and cherries (if using) in the pan around the pork. Drizzle with a little oil.

To make the stuffing, heat the oil and butter in a large, heavy skillet. When the foam subsides, add the onion and celery and cook for 4–5 minutes, until soft. Add the apple or pear and rosemary and cook for another minute. Cut or tear the bread into a large bowl and add the onion mixture. Pour the stock overtop and toss with your hands to combine. Season with salt and pepper. Mound the stuffing in the middle of the crown roast; place whatever doesn't fit into a small baking dish.

Preheat the oven to 325°F (160°C). Roast the pork for 2–2½ hours, covering the stuffing and bones with foil if they are browning too quickly, until it reaches an internal temperature of 155°F–160°F (68°C–71°C). (Insert your thermometer into the meatiest part of the roast, ensuring it doesn't touch the bone.) The extra dish of stuffing can be roasted alongside the pork, but will only need about an hour.

Tent the roast with foil and let rest for 20 minutes. Cut between each bone to make a thick chop, and serve with roasted apples or pears and stuffing.

SERVES 10

apple rosemary-glazed ribs

- 2 racks pork back or side ribs
- 1 Tbsp (15 mL) finely chopped fresh rosemary
- Salt and freshly ground black pepper
- 2 cups (500 mL) apple cider
- 1 Tbsp (15 mL) soy sauce (optional)

Reduced apple cider is perfect for glazing pork ribs. Baking them for a long time at a low temperature allows the tough connective tissues to break down, making them ultra-tender. Finishing them with the apple glaze keeps it from burning.

Preheat the oven to 300°F (150°C).

Place the ribs on a large rimmed foil-lined baking sheet, sprinkle with rosemary, salt, and pepper, and cover tightly with foil. Roast for 2½ hours, until the meat is very tender.

Meanwhile, heat the apple cider in a small saucepan set over medium-high heat and simmer until it's reduced to about a quarter and has the consistency of runny syrup. Set aside to cool and stir in the soy sauce.

Turn the oven up to 400°F (200°C) and brush the reduced cider all over the ribs. Return to the oven for 20 minutes, brushing again once or twice, until the ribs are dark and sticky.

SERVES 6

peach thai chicken thighs

- 8 skinless chicken thighs (with or without the bone)
- 1 cup (250 mL) salsa
- 1 peach or 2–3 apricots, sliced
- ¼–½ cup (60–125 mL) peanut butter
- 2 Tbsp (30 mL) soy sauce
- 1 Tbsp (15 mL) lime juice
- 2 tsp (10 mL) grated fresh ginger
- Chopped fresh cilantro, for serving

This is one of the simplest recipes ever, and it just happens to produce one of the most delicious meals. Fresh peaches or apricots add sweetness and tang; slice them right into the slow cooker along with inexpensive chicken thighs, salsa for sauce and heat, and peanut butter for richness. If you don't have a slow cooker, simmer the ingredients in a covered pot in the oven for 2–3 hours, adding a splash of water or stock if the dish seems dry.

Combine all the ingredients in a slow cooker, cover, and cook on low for 6 hours, stirring once if you have the chance.

Serve warm over rice and topped with fresh cilantro.

SERVES 4

roast chicken with cider glaze & peaches

- 1 cup (250 mL) apple cider (optional)
- 1 whole roasting chicken (about 3–4 lb/ 1.5–1.8 kg)
- Canola oil, for cooking
- 2 sprigs fresh thyme, plus more (optional) for stuffing
- 2–3 sprigs fresh rosemary and/or parsley (optional)
- Salt and freshly ground black pepper
- 1–2 peaches, halved or sliced, or apple wedges

Chicken is always happy to be bathed in a sticky glaze as it roasts. Sliced peaches simmered alongside cook to a soft, sludgy consistency and are delicious with the roast chicken.

If you're making the glaze, heat the apple cider in a small saucepan set over medium-high heat and simmer until it's reduced to about a quarter and has the consistency of runny syrup.

Pat a whole roasting chicken dry with paper towel and place in a baking dish or cast iron skillet. Drizzle with oil and rub all over the skin to coat. Sprinkle with the leaves pulled from a few sprigs of thyme and some salt and pepper. If you like, tuck a small handful of fresh thyme, rosemary, and/or parsley into the cavity.

Roast at 425°F (220°C) for 1 hour for a 3–4 lb (1.5–1.8 kg) bird, or 1½ hours if you have a larger 5–6 lb (2.2–2.7 kg) bird. Halfway through the cooking time, pull the chicken out of the oven, brush it all over with the reduced cider, and add the peaches or apples to the pan and stir them around in the pan drippings before returning the chicken to the oven. It's done when the juices run clear and the joints wiggle in their sockets.

Let the chicken rest for 10 minutes before carving. Serve with the soft roasted fruit.

SERVES 4

turkey apple sage meatloaf

- 1 cup (250 mL) dry breadcrumbs, crushed crackers, or croutons
- ½ cup (125 mL) milk, half & half cream, or apple cider
- 2 lb (1 kg) ground turkey
- 1 medium onion, coarsely grated
- 1 large apple, coarsely grated (don't bother peeling it)
- 1 large egg
- 2 tsp (10 mL) dry or 2 Tbsp (30 mL) chopped fresh sage
- ½ tsp (2 mL) salt

This moist meatloaf has all the flavours of turkey dinner, but it's easier to carve. The grated apple adds moisture, sweetness, and flavour. If you like, brush the loaf with oil as it cooks to help give it a golden crust; before serving, brush with the pan drippings for more colour.

Preheat the oven to 375°F (190°C).

In a large bowl, combine the breadcrumbs and milk and let sit for 5 minutes to soften. Add the remaining ingredients and mix with your hands until just combined.

Pat into a loaf pan or shape into a free-form loaf on a rimmed baking sheet. Bake for an hour or until just cooked through. (If you have a meat thermometer, the internal temperature should read 160°F/71°C.) Let rest for a few minutes before slicing.

SERVES 6

braised beef short ribs with cherries

Canola oil, for cooking
2 lb (1 kg) beef or bison short ribs (about 6)
Salt and freshly ground black pepper
1 small onion, halved and thinly sliced
3 garlic cloves, crushed
1–2 cups (250–500 mL) cherries, pitted
¼ cup (60 mL) balsamic vinegar
1 cup (250 mL) red wine (optional)
2–3 cups (500–750 mL) beef or chicken stock
Salt, to taste

Beef short ribs are simple to braise; browning them first adds a ton of flavour. The result is fall-off-the-bone meat and lots of delicious gravy to serve over mashed potatoes or buttered noodles.

Preheat the oven to 300°F (150°C).

Heat a drizzle of oil in a heavy skillet, braising dish, or oven-proof pot set over medium-high heat. Season the ribs with salt and pepper and brown on all sides; set aside.

Add the onion to the pan and cook for a few minutes, stirring often, until it starts to soften. Add the garlic and cook for another minute. Add the cherries and pour in the balsamic vinegar. Cook for a minute, scraping up the browned bits from the bottom of the pan.

Return the browned ribs to the pot and add the wine (if using) and enough stock to come about halfway up the sides of the ribs. Cover and cook for 3 hours, until the meat is very tender. Remove the ribs from the pot, skim off any excess fat, and season with salt. If you like, simmer the sauce on the stovetop to thicken and reduce it slightly before returning the ribs to the pot.

Serve over mashed potatoes or buttered noodles to catch the drips.

SERVES 6

sausage smothered in red cabbage with apples & cherries

Canola oil, for cooking
1 Tbsp (15 mL) butter
1 lb (500 g) kielbasa or garlic sausage, cut into ½-inch (1 cm) pieces
1 small onion, chopped
1 small or ½ medium head red cabbage, shredded
1 apple, cored and diced
2 cups (500 mL) cherries, pitted and halved
¼ cup (60 mL) packed brown sugar
2 Tbsp (30 mL) balsamic vinegar
Salt and freshly ground black pepper

A thick link of kielbasa or garlic sausage simmered with apples, cherries, and red cabbage makes a tasty one-dish dinner.

In a large, heavy skillet, heat a drizzle of oil along with the butter over medium-high heat. Add the sausage and cook until it starts to brown.

Add the onion and cook for a few minutes, until it softens. Add the cabbage and apple and cook, stirring often and covering with a lid, until soft. Add the cherries, brown sugar, and balsamic vinegar and continue cooking, stirring often, until thickened and softened.

Season with salt and pepper and serve warm.

SERVES 4

PIES, GALETTES & TARTS

classic apple pie

PASTRY:

2 cups (500 mL) all-purpose flour
2 tsp (10 mL) sugar
¼ tsp (1 mL) salt
½ cup (125 mL) butter, cut into pieces
½ cup (125 mL) lard, cut into pieces
⅓ cup (85 mL) cold water
1 large egg

FILLING:

5–6 large apples, peeled, cored, and thinly sliced
1 Tbsp (15 mL) lemon juice
⅔ cup (160 mL) sugar
2 Tbsp (30 mL) all-purpose flour
1 tsp (5 mL) cinnamon

Cream or milk, for brushing (optional)
Coarse sugar, for sprinkling (optional)

What's better when apples are in season than a high-topped apple pie? I like to use a combination of tart apples for a more complex flavour. They will shrink as they cook, leaving a high domed crust to crack through. If you like, make an all-butter crust using 1 cup (250 mL) of butter rather than butter and lard.

In a large bowl, stir together the flour, sugar, and salt. Add the butter and lard and blend with a pastry blender or a fork until the mixture is well blended and crumbly, with pieces of fat no bigger than a pea.

In a small bowl or measuring cup, stir together the water and egg with a fork. Add to the flour mixture and stir just until the dough comes together. Cut in half, making one piece slightly bigger than the other. Shape each into a disc and let rest for 20 minutes.

Preheat the oven to 425°F (220°C).

On a lightly floured surface, roll the larger piece of pastry into an 11- to 12-inch (28–30 cm) circle. Transfer to a pie plate and press to fit, letting the sides hang over the edge.

Slice the apples into a large bowl and sprinkle with lemon juice. Add the sugar, flour, and cinnamon and toss to coat, then pile into the pie shell.

Roll out the other half of the dough, making it slightly larger than the top of the pie (about 10 inches/25 cm) and place over the apples, pressing to seal around the edge. Trim (scissors work well for this) and crimp the edge, or just fold the edge haphazardly up around the pie—it will still look great.

If you like, brush the top with cream and/or sprinkle with sugar. Cut a few slits in the top to help the steam escape. Bake for 15 minutes, then reduce the heat to 375°F (190°C) and bake for another hour, or until golden and bubbly.

SERVES 8

apple turnover slab pie

FILLING:

2 Tbsp (30 mL) butter
2 tart apples, cored and thinly sliced
3 Tbsp (45 mL) dark brown sugar
½ tsp (2 mL) cinnamon

PASTRY:

½ package puff pastry, thawed but cold
1 egg, lightly beaten
Coarse sugar, for sprinkling (optional)

Like a long rectangular turnover, this pie is easy to assemble and is served in wedges or slices, like strudel. Sautéing the apples first caramelizes them, intensifying their flavour and cooking off any excess moisture that might otherwise make your pie soggy. This is an easy recipe to double; just use a whole package of puff pastry and cook twice the quantity of apples.

Preheat the oven to 400°F (200°C).

Set a large, heavy skillet over medium-high heat and add the butter. When the foaming subsides, add the apples and cook for 5–6 minutes, until tender and starting to turn golden. Add the brown sugar and cinnamon and cook, stirring, for another minute. Remove from heat and set aside to cool slightly.

On a lightly floured surface, roll out the puff pastry to about a 9- × 11-inch (23 × 28 cm) rectangle (or unroll if it's already rolled out) and transfer to a parchment-lined baking sheet.

Cut the pastry in half lengthwise and brush the edges of one half with beaten egg. Spread the sautéed apples in a strip down the middle, leaving about ½ inch (1 cm) around each side.

Top with the second piece of pastry (you may have to stretch it a little with your fingers) and press around the edges to seal. Press down around the edges with the tines of a fork. Brush the pastry all over with beaten egg and, if you like, sprinkle with coarse sugar. Cut a few slashes in the top with a sharp knife.

Bake for 20 minutes or until deep golden. Let cool slightly before cutting into slices or wedges.

SERVES 6

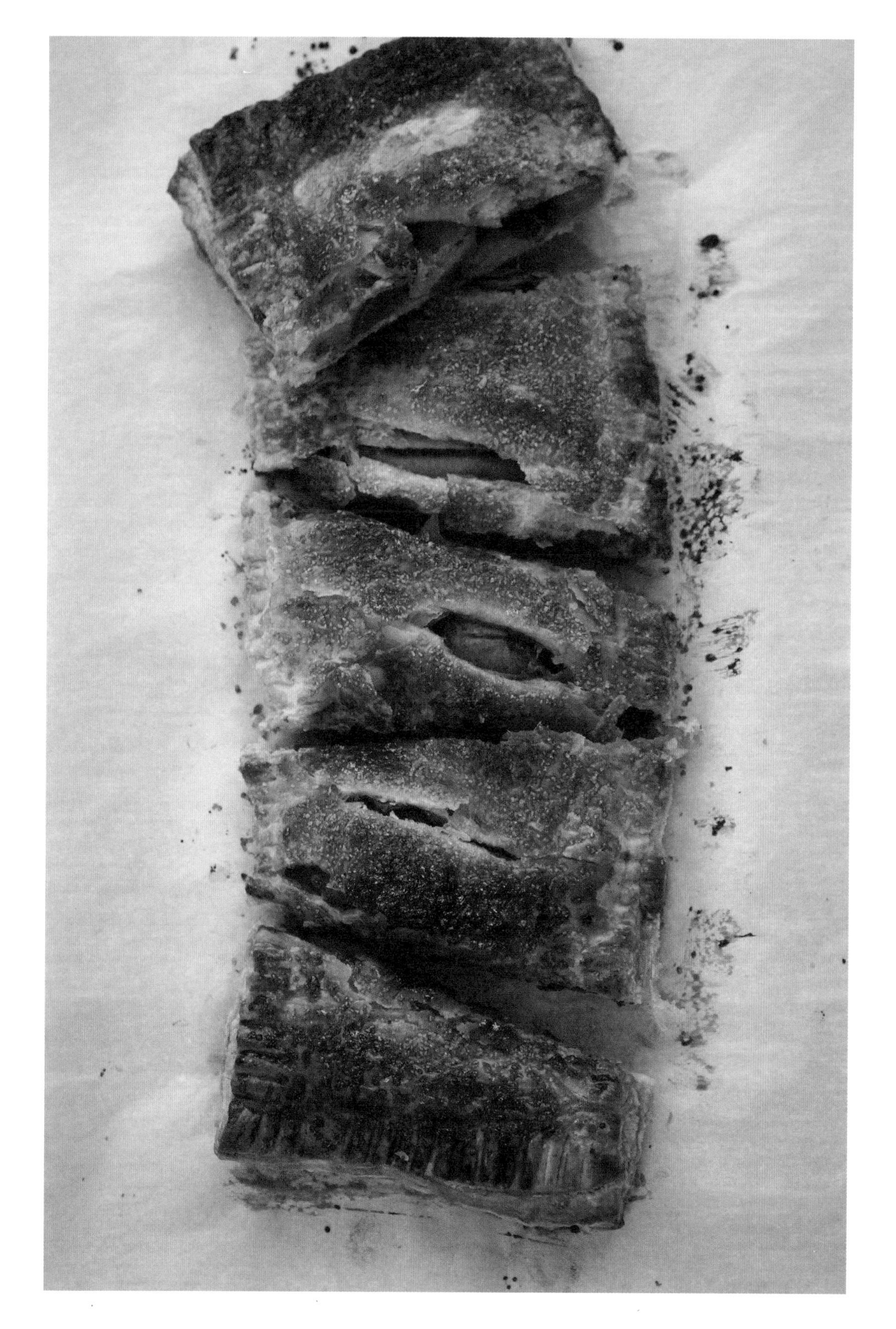

pear tarte tatin

FILLING:

- 1 cup (250 mL) sugar
- ⅓ cup (85 mL) butter
- 1 Tbsp (15 mL) lemon juice
- 2 lb (1 kg) firm pears, peeled, cored, and halved lengthwise (about 4 pears)

PASTRY:

- ½ package puff pastry, thawed but cold, or pastry for a single-crust pie (see page 121; use one of the discs)

An upside-down pie, tarte tatin is made by caramelizing apples or pears before topping them with pastry and baking the whole thing. It's then inverted onto a plate, caramelized juices and all, and served in wedges with whipped cream or ice cream.

Preheat the oven to 425°F (220°C).

In a heavy cast iron skillet, combine the sugar, butter, and lemon juice over medium-high heat. Cook for about 5 minutes, stirring until it turns deep golden. Remove from heat.

To fan the pears, place core side down on a cutting board and cut into 4 lengthwise slices, leaving the pointy end attached. Arrange cut side up in the pan, fanning them slightly and placing them close together (the pears will shrink as they cook).

Roll the pastry out until it's about as big (or a little bigger) than the skillet; cover the pears and tuck the edge in around them. Cut a few slits in the top and bake for 20–25 minutes, until golden.

Carefully invert the tarte tatin onto a plate while it's still warm.

Pears tend to be juicier, and make for runnier caramel, so anticipate some drips—or substitute any variety of tart apples.

SERVES 6–8

sour cream peach custard streusel pie

PASTRY:

Pastry for a single-crust pie (see page 121; use one of the discs)

FILLING:

1 cup (250 mL) sugar
1 cup (250 mL) sour cream
½ cup (125 mL) heavy (whipping) cream
3 large egg yolks
¼ cup (60 mL) all-purpose flour
1 tsp (5 mL) vanilla
¼ tsp (1 mL) salt
2 cups (500 mL) sliced peaches, fresh or frozen, peeled or not

STREUSEL:

½ cup (125 mL) all-purpose flour
½ cup (125 mL) brown sugar
¼ cup (60 mL) butter
¼ cup (60 mL) sliced almonds or chopped pecans

Peach custard pies are classic, but nectarines and apricots make delicious alternatives. The custard binds slices together; the streusel adds a sweet crunch on top.

Preheat the oven to 425°F (220°C).

On a lightly floured surface, roll the pastry out into an 11-inch (28 cm) circle. Fit it into a 9-inch (23 cm) pie plate, letting the edge hang over.

In a medium bowl, whisk together the sugar, sour cream, whipping cream, egg yolks, flour, vanilla, and salt. Arrange the peach slices in concentric circles in the bottom of the pie and pour the custard overtop.

Bake for 30 minutes, then turn the oven down to 350°F (180°C). Meanwhile, in a medium bowl, blend together the flour, brown sugar, butter, and almonds, mixing with a fork or your fingers until crumbly.

Sprinkle over the pie and bake for another 20 minutes, until the streusel is golden.

Cool the pie on a wire rack, or serve warm.

SERVES 8

cherry pie

Pastry for a double-crust pie (see page 121)

FILLING:
5 cups (1.25 L) cherries, pitted
1 Tbsp (15 mL) lemon juice
1 cup (250 mL) sugar
¼ cup (60 mL) cornstarch

Cream or milk, for brushing (optional)
Coarse sugar, for sprinkling (optional)

When cherries are in, homemade pie is a must. If you don't have a cherry pitter, try setting them one at a time on top of an open bottle and pitting them by pushing a sturdy straw through the middle, depositing each pit into the bottle.

In a large bowl, stir together the flour, sugar, and salt. Add thc butter and lard and blend with a pastry blender or a fork until the mixture is well blended and crumbly, with pieces of fat no bigger than a pea.

In a small bowl or measuring cup, whisk together the water and egg with a fork. Add to the flour mixture and stir just until the dough comes together. Cut in half, making one piece slightly bigger than the other. Shape each into a disc and let rest for 20 minutes.

Meanwhile, preheat the oven to 400°F (200°C). In a medium bowl, toss the cherries and lemon juice. Stir together the sugar and cornstarch and shake over the berries; toss to coat.

On a lightly floured surface, roll the larger piece of pastry into a circle about an inch (2.5 cm) wider in diameter than your pie plate. Transfer to the plate and press to fit, letting the sides hang over the edge.

Put the cherries into the shell and roll out the second piece of pastry to about the same size as the top of the pie. Cut into strips and lay across the top of the pie, making a lattice if you like, or just place them haphazardly across the top, allowing some space for steam to escape. Trim and crimp the edge and, if you like, brush the top with cream and/or sprinkle with sugar.

Bake for 15 minutes, then reduce the heat to 375°F (190°C) and bake for another hour or until golden and bubbly.

SERVES 8

stone fruit galette

PASTRY:
1⅓ cups (330 mL) all-purpose flour
1 tsp (5 mL) sugar
Pinch salt
½ cup (125 mL) butter, chilled and cut into pieces
¼ cup (60 mL) cold water

FILLING:
1 peach or nectarine, pitted and sliced
3 plums or apricots, pitted and sliced
1 cup (250 mL) blueberries or pitted, halved cherries
1 cup (250 mL) blackberries or raspberries
1 Tbsp (15 mL) lemon juice
½ cup (125 mL) sugar
2 Tbsp (30 mL) all-purpose flour

Milk or cream, for brushing (optional)
Sugar, for sprinkling (optional)

A galette is a free-form pie baked on a cookie sheet. There's no pressure to fit pastry into a pie plate—just roll out the dough, pile it with fruit, then fold up the edges to keep any sticky juices from escaping. It's the perfect vehicle for stone fruits, which go well with berries to fill in the gaps.

In a medium bowl, combine the flour, sugar, and salt. Cut in the butter with a pastry blender or fork until it's well combined, with lumps of fat the size of a pea. Add the water and stir until the dough comes together. Gather into a ball and let it rest for 20 minutes, then roll out into a 10- to 12-inch (25–30 cm) circle. Transfer to a parchment-lined baking sheet.

Preheat the oven to 375°F (190°C).

Toss all the fruit in a large bowl with the lemon juice. Stir together the sugar and flour and sprinkle over the fruit, toss to coat, and mound into the middle of the pastry, spreading it out to within an inch or two of the edge.

Fold the edge of the pastry over wherever it wants to rest, enclosing the fruit. If you like, brush the edge of the pastry with milk or cream and/or sprinkle with sugar.

Bake for 40–45 minutes, until the fruit is bubbly and the crust is golden. Let cool to at least lukewarm before you cut into it.

Serve warm with ice cream or whipped cream.

SERVES 8

maple apple galette

PASTRY:

1⅓ cups (330 mL) all-purpose or whole wheat flour, or some of each
1 Tbsp (15 mL) brown sugar
Pinch salt
½ cup (125 mL) butter, chilled and cut into pieces
¼ cup (60 mL) cold water

FILLING:

3 tart apples, cored and thinly sliced
¼ cup (60 mL) sugar
1 tsp (5 mL) cinnamon
2 Tbsp (30 mL) pure maple syrup

If the thought of attempting an apple pie is intimidating, a galette is a good place to start. I like using whole wheat flour in the pastry for a nutty, tweedy crust.

Preheat the oven to 400°F (200°C).

In a medium bowl, combine the flour, brown sugar, and salt. Cut in the butter with a pastry blender or fork until it's well combined, with lumps of fat the size of a pea.

Add the water and stir until the dough comes together. Gather into a ball and let it rest for 20 minutes, then roll out into a 10- to 12-inch (25–30 cm) circle. Transfer to a parchment-lined baking sheet.

Thinly slice the apples into a bowl, toss with sugar and cinnamon, and pile into the middle of the pastry, leaving an inch around the edge. Fold the pastry over wherever it wants to rest, enclosing the fruit.

Drizzle maple syrup overtop and bake for 1 hour, until tender and golden. Let cool slightly before cutting into wedges to serve.

SERVES 8

puff pastry plum tarts

½–1 package puff pastry, thawed but cold
¼ cup (60 mL) sugar
2–3 Tbsp (30–45 mL) sliced almonds
2–3 plums, pitted and thinly sliced
1 egg, beaten (optional)

Thawed puff pastry is easy to roll, top with juicy fruit, and bake into individual tarts that can be served in the morning as a sort of extra-fruity Danish, or for dessert with vanilla ice cream. The recipe is easily doubled and works well with fresh apricots, too. If you like, spread a layer of sweetened cream cheese or mascarpone on the pastry and lay the sliced fruit on top.

Preheat the oven to 425°F (220°C).

On a lightly floured surface, roll the pastry out ¼-inch (6 mm) thick (or less) and cut into 3- to 4-inch (8–10 cm) squares.

Place the squares on a parchment-lined baking sheet, sprinkle with about half the sugar and all of the almonds, then top with thinly sliced plums. Fold the edges over about ½ inch (1 cm) and, if you like, brush with some beaten egg.

Sprinkle with the remaining sugar and bake for 20 minutes or until golden. Serve warm.

MAKES 4–6 TARTS

CAKES

stone fruit buckle

CAKE:

½ cup (125 mL) butter, at room temperature
¾ cup (185 mL) sugar
1 large egg
1 tsp (5 mL) vanilla
1½ cups (375 mL) all-purpose flour
1½ tsp (7 mL) baking powder
¼ tsp (1 mL) salt
1 cup (250 mL) milk
4–5 plums, 3–4 apricots, or 2–3 peaches, pitted and quartered

CRUMBLE:

½ cup (125 mL) packed brown sugar
¼ cup (60 mL) all-purpose flour
¼ cup (60 mL) butter, at room temperature
¼ tsp (1 mL) cinnamon

A buckle is a dense coffee cake with a crumble topping. It makes a perfect vehicle for any kind of fruit in season, but works particularly well with tart, juicy stone fruits.

Preheat the oven to 350°F (180°C) and butter an 8- × 8-inch (20 × 20 cm) pan or line it with parchment.

In a large bowl, beat the butter and sugar until pale and light, then beat in the egg and vanilla.

In a small bowl, stir together the flour, baking powder, and salt. Add half to the butter mixture, stirring just until combined. Add the milk, then the rest of the flour mixture, stirring just until blended. Scrape into the prepared pan. Place the fruit in rows or scatter haphazardly over the top of the batter.

In a medium bowl, combine the brown sugar, flour, butter, and cinnamon and blend with a fork or your fingers until crumbly. Sprinkle over the fruit, squeezing as you go to create larger clumps.

Bake for 45–50 minutes, until the cake is golden and springy to the touch. Serve warm.

SERVES 9

caramel apple sour cream coffee cake

CAKE:

- ¼ cup (60 mL) butter, at room temperature, or canola oil
- ½ cup (125 mL) sugar
- ⅓ cup (85 mL) packed brown sugar
- 2 large eggs
- 1 tsp (5 mL) vanilla
- 1¾ cups (435 mL) all-purpose flour
- 2 tsp (10 mL) cinnamon
- 1 tsp (5 mL) ground ginger
- 1½ tsp (7 mL) baking powder
- ½ tsp (2 mL) baking soda
- ¼ tsp (1 mL) salt
- 1 cup (250 mL) sour cream or plain yogurt
- 2 apples, cored and sliced

CARAMEL SAUCE:

- ½ cup (125 mL) packed light brown sugar
- ¼ cup (60 mL) heavy (whipping) cream
- 2 Tbsp (30 mL) butter

Caramel and apples join forces in this dense, moist cake. It's baked in a tube pan, the kind you might use for an angel food cake. If you don't have one, use a Bundt pan.

Preheat the oven to 350°F (180°C) and spray a 10-inch (25 cm) tube pan with nonstick spray.

In a large bowl, beat the butter, sugar, and brown sugar until well blended. Beat in the eggs and vanilla.

In a medium bowl, whisk together the flour, cinnamon, ginger, baking powder, baking soda, and salt. Add about a third to the butter mixture and stir by hand or beat with a hand-held mixer on low speed just until blended. Add half the sour cream or yogurt, another third of the dry ingredients, the rest of the sour cream or yogurt, and the rest of the dry ingredients, stirring after each addition just until combined. Scrape the batter into the pan and arrange the apple slices tightly on top.

To make the sauce, bring the brown sugar, cream, and butter to a simmer in a small saucepan set over medium-high heat, whisking often. Remove from heat and cool slightly, then drizzle over the cake.

Bake for 45 minutes, until the cake is springy to the touch. Cool in the pan on a wire rack.

SERVES 8–12

upside-down pear gingerbread

TOPPING:

2 Tbsp (30 mL) butter
2 Tbsp (30 mL) honey or corn syrup
⅓ cup (85 mL) packed brown sugar
1–2 ripe but firm pears or tart apples, peeled, cored, and thinly sliced

GINGERBREAD:

¼ cup (60 mL) butter, at room temperature
½ cup (125 mL) packed brown sugar
1 large egg
½ cup (125 mL) buttermilk
¼ cup (60 mL) dark molasses
1 Tbsp (15 mL) grated fresh ginger, or 1 tsp (5 mL) ground ginger
1 cup (250 mL) all-purpose flour
1 tsp (5 mL) baking soda
½ tsp (2 mL) cinnamon
¼ tsp (1 mL) allspice or pumpkin pie spice (optional)
¼ tsp (1 mL) salt

Pears and gingerbread are a perfect pairing. This is the Thanksgiving dessert of choice in our family—it even beats out pumpkin pie. Bonus: Upside-down cakes require no decorating, only a dollop of whipped cream.

Preheat the oven to 350°F (180°C).

To make the topping, melt the butter, honey or corn syrup, and brown sugar in a small saucepan over medium heat, stirring until smooth. Pour the mixture over the bottom of a 9-inch (23 cm) pan and arrange the pear slices on top, placing them tightly together; they shrink a bit as they cook, so you can even get away with overlapping them.

To make the gingerbread, beat the butter and brown sugar in a medium bowl until well blended. Add the egg, buttermilk, molasses, and ginger and beat until thoroughly combined.

In a small bowl, stir together the flour, baking soda, cinnamon, allspice or pumpkin pie spice (if using), and salt. Add the dry ingredients to the egg mixture and stir by hand or beat with a hand-held mixer on low speed just until combined. Pour the batter over the sliced pears.

Bake the cake for about 40 minutes, until the top is springy to the touch. Let it stand for 5 minutes, then run a knife around the edge of the cake and invert it onto a plate while it's still warm. If it cools too much and sticks to the pan, warm it in the oven again before you try to invert it.

Serve warm with whipped cream.

SERVES 8

cherry & peach upside-down sour cream cake

TOPPING:

½ cup (125 mL) butter
¾ cup (185 mL) packed brown sugar
1 Tbsp (15 mL) honey or pure maple syrup
2–3 peaches, pitted, peeled, and cut into ½-inch (1 cm) slices
½–1 cup (125–250 mL) fresh cherries, pitted and halved

CAKE:

2¼ cups (560 mL) all-purpose flour
¾ cup (185 mL) sugar
1 Tbsp (15 mL) baking powder
½ tsp (2 mL) baking soda
¼ tsp (1 mL) salt
1 cup (250 mL) sour cream or plain yogurt
2 large eggs
¼ cup (60 mL) milk
¼ cup (60 mL) canola oil

Although most of us associate upside-down cakes with pineapple, juicy peaches come a close second. Tuck cherries in the gaps between slices, or use peach halves and stick a cherry where the pit used to be.

Preheat the oven to 350°F (180°C).

Set a 9- or 10-inch (23 or 25 cm) cast iron skillet over medium-high heat and melt the butter with the brown sugar and honey or syrup, whisking until smooth. Remove the pan from the heat and place the peach pieces on the bottom, fitting them tightly in concentric circles. Tuck cherries into any spaces.

In a large bowl, stir together the flour, sugar, baking powder, baking soda, and salt. In a medium bowl, whisk together the sour cream or yogurt, eggs, milk, and oil; add to the dry ingredients and stir just until combined.

Spread the batter over the fruit and bake for 40 minutes, or until golden and springy to the touch. Let cool in the pan for 5–10 minutes, then run a thin knife around the edge and invert onto a plate while it's still warm. If any pieces of fruit stick, pull them out and put them back on the top of the cake.

SERVES 8–12

cherry vanilla bundt cake

1 cup (250 mL) butter, at room temperature
2 cups (500 mL) sugar
¼ cup (60 mL) canola or other vegetable oil
1 Tbsp (15 mL) vanilla
4 large eggs
3¾ cups (935 mL) all-purpose flour, divided
2 tsp (10 mL) baking powder
½ tsp (2 mL) salt
1 cup (250 mL) milk
3 cups (750 mL) cherries, pitted and halved

This is a variation, using fresh cherries, of a candied cherry cake recipe that Canadian music icon Anne Murray has shared in the past. For an almond-scented version, swap the vanilla for almond extract.

Preheat the oven to 325°F (160°C).

In a large bowl, beat the butter, sugar, oil, and vanilla for 2–3 minutes, until pale and light. Beat in the eggs, one at a time.

Combine 3½ cups (875 mL) of the flour with the baking powder and salt; add to the butter mixture in three additions, alternating with the milk in two additions. Toss the cherries with the remaining flour and stir into the batter.

Pour into a well-greased Bundt pan and bake for 1–1½ hours or until golden and the top is springy to the touch. Let cool for a few minutes in the pan, then turn out onto a wire rack to cool completely.

SERVES 16

stone fruit spoon cake

- 2–3 peaches or nectarines, cored and sliced
- 2 plums, pitted and sliced, or 1 cup halved cherries
- ¾ cup + 3 Tbsp (220 mL) sugar
- pinch cinnamon
- ½ cup (125 mL) butter, melted
- 2 large eggs
- 1 cup (250 mL) all-purpose flour
- ¼ (1 mL) tsp salt

This is one of those recipes that can be called into service no matter what type of fruit is in season (or stashed away in the freezer). In winter, apples and pears are delicious, spiked with cinnamon; in summer and fall, try thickly sliced stone fruits like peaches, plums, apricots and cherries.

Preheat the oven to 350°F and butter a pie plate.

Toss the fruit in the pie plate with about 2 Tbsp of the sugar and the cinnamon; spread out in a single layer.

In a medium bowl, stir together the melted butter and ¾ cup of the sugar; stir in the eggs, and then the flour and salt. Pour over the fruit, smoothing the top, and sprinkle with the last tablespoon of sugar.

Bake for 40–45 minutes, until the top is golden and crusty and the juices are bubbling around the edges. Serve warm, by the spoonful, with vanilla ice cream or whipped cream, or for breakfast with thick vanilla yogurt.

SERVES 8

spiced pear bundt cake

- 3 cups (750 mL) all-purpose flour
- ¾ cup (185 mL) packed brown sugar
- 1½ tsp (7 mL) baking soda
- 2 tsp (10 mL) cinnamon
- 1 tsp (5 mL) ground ginger
- ½ tsp (2 mL) allspice
- ½ tsp (2 mL) salt
- 3 very ripe pears
- ½ cup (125 mL) canola oil
- ¾ cup (185 mL) sugar
- 3 large eggs
- 2 tsp (10 mL) vanilla
- ½ cup (125 mL) chopped walnuts or pecans (optional)

This warm spiced cake is reminiscent of a light gingerbread and is delicious served in wedges with tea or coffee. If you like, stir in some chopped candied ginger, or slather the cake with cream cheese frosting.

Preheat the oven to 350°F (180°C).

In a large bowl, whisk together the flour, brown sugar, baking soda, cinnamon, ginger, allspice, and salt; set aside. Coarsely grate two of the pears (don't bother peeling them) onto a plate; core and dice the third.

In a medium bowl, whisk together the oil, sugar, eggs, and vanilla; add to the dry ingredients along with the grated pears and any juices that have collected on the plate, and stir until the batter is almost combined. Add the chopped pear and nuts, if you're using them, and stir just until blended.

Scrape the batter into a greased Bundt pan and bake for an hour or until deep golden, domed on top, and springy to the touch. Let cool for a few minutes before inverting onto a plate or wire rack to cool.

SERVES 16

black forest cupcakes

CUPCAKES:

1¾ cups (435 mL) all-purpose flour, or half all-purpose, half whole wheat
1 cup (250 mL) packed brown sugar
½ cup (125 mL) cocoa
1 tsp (5 mL) baking powder
1 tsp (5 mL) baking soda
½ tsp (2 mL) salt
1 cup (250 mL) milk
½ cup (125 mL) canola oil
2 large eggs
2 tsp (10 mL) vanilla
1 cup (250 mL) strong coffee

FILLING:

2 cups (500 mL) fresh or frozen cherries, pitted
½ cup (125 mL) sugar
2 Tbsp (30 mL) cornstarch

TOPPING:

1 cup (250 mL) heavy (whipping) cream
1 Tbsp (15 mL) sugar
½ tsp (2 mL) vanilla
Chocolate shavings or extra cherries (optional)

Dense chocolate cupcakes make perfect vehicles for cherry filling. Top them with a dollop of whipped cream for a far simpler version of Black Forest cake. For a pretty presentation, spoon the whipped cream into a zip-lock bag, cut off one corner, and pipe it out onto each cupcake.

Preheat the oven to 350°F (180°C).

In a large bowl, whisk together the flour, brown sugar, cocoa, baking powder, baking soda, and salt, breaking up any lumps of brown sugar and cocoa. Add the milk, oil, eggs, and vanilla and whisk to combine. Add the coffee and stir until well blended and smooth.

Divide the batter among 12–18 paper-lined muffin cups, filling them three-quarters full, and bake for 25 minutes or until the tops are springy to the touch. Set aside on a wire rack to cool completely.

Meanwhile, combine the cherries, sugar, and cornstarch in a medium saucepan set over medium heat, and bring to a simmer. Cook until bubbling and thickened; remove from heat and set aside to cool.

With a sharp knife, cut a small piece out of the top of each cupcake. (If you cut in a circle with the knife pointed in, you end up with a little cone-shaped chunk of cake.) Fill each cupcake with a small spoonful of filling, then replace the piece of cake you cut out. (You may have to break off the pointy end to accommodate the filling.)

Whip the cream with the sugar and vanilla until stiff peaks form. Spoon onto the cupcakes, or spoon into a large zip-lock bag, snip off one corner, and pipe over the cupcakes. Top with cherries and/or chocolate shavings, if you like.

MAKES 1–1½ DOZEN CUPCAKES

apple pie cheesecake

CRUST:

1 cup (250 mL) all-purpose flour
¼ cup (60 mL) packed brown sugar
½ cup (125 mL) butter, at room temperature

FILLING:

Two 8 oz (250 g) packages cream cheese, at room temperature
½ cup (125 mL) sugar
2 large eggs
1 tsp (5 mL) vanilla

TOPPING:

2 tart apples, cored and thinly sliced
½ cup (125 mL) sugar
1 tsp (5 mL) cinnamon

I don't know Pat Ryer, but on the Internet I came across a recipe for apple pie cheesecake credited to her, and it's a brilliant, beautiful combination; spiced apples and creamy cheesecake make a delicious combo. As far as cheesecakes go, it's a simple one to make, and I imagine it would be just as good with pears. Thanks Pat!

Preheat the oven to 400°F (200°C).

In a small bowl, combine the flour, sugar, and butter, blending with a fork until the mixture is well blended. Press the crumbs into the bottom and about an inch (2.5 cm) up the sides of a buttered 9-inch (23 cm) springform pan.

In a large bowl, beat the cream cheese and sugar until smooth. Beat in the eggs one at a time, then beat in the vanilla. Pour over the crust.

In a small bowl (use the one for the crust), toss the apples with the sugar and cinnamon and scatter over the top of the cheesecake. Bake for 12 minutes, then reduce the heat to 375°F (190°C) and bake for another 30–35 minutes, until puffed and golden but slightly jiggly; it will firm up as it cools.

Let cool in the pan, then refrigerate for a few hours or overnight.

SERVES 1

COOKIES, CRISPS & DESSERTS

spiced pear lassy mogs

- ¾ cup (185 mL) butter, at room temperature
- ¾ cup (185 mL) packed brown sugar
- ¼ cup (60 mL) dark molasses (not blackstrap)
- 1 large egg
- 1 tsp (5 mL) vanilla
- 2 cups (500 mL) all-purpose flour
- 2 tsp (10 mL) cinnamon
- 1 tsp (5 mL) ground ginger
- Pinch allspice (optional)
- ¼ tsp (1 mL) salt
- 1 very ripe pear, coarsely grated (don't bother peeling it)
- ½–1 cup (125–250 mL) chopped dates
- ½ cup (125 mL) chopped pecans

A traditional soft gingerbread cookie from Atlantic Canada, "lassy" refers to molasses. Grated overripe pear adds sweetness, moisture, and a wonderful cakey texture. Sandwiching cream cheese frosting, these would make delicious whoopie pies.

Preheat the oven to 350°F (180°C).

In a large bowl, beat the butter and brown sugar for a minute or two, until fluffy. Beat in the molasses, egg, and vanilla; don't worry if it looks like it's separating.

In a small bowl, stir together the flour, cinnamon, ginger, allspice (if using), and salt. Add to the butter mixture along with the grated pear, and stir or beat with a hand-held mixer on low speed just until combined. Stir in the dates and pecans.

Drop by the large spoonful (or use an ice cream scoop for more uniform cookies) onto a parchment-lined baking sheet and bake for 14–16 minutes, until set and just springy to the touch. Transfer to a wire rack to cool.

MAKES 2 DOZEN COOKIES

chewy apple oatmeal cookies

¼ cup (60 mL) butter, at room temperature
¼ cup (60 mL) canola oil
½ cup (125 mL) packed brown sugar
½ tsp (2 mL) cinnamon
1 large egg
1 tsp (5 mL) vanilla
1 cup (250 mL) all-purpose flour
1 cup (250 mL) old-fashioned oats
1 tsp (5 mL) baking soda
½ tsp (2 mL) salt
1 tart apple, cored and coarsely chopped (don't bother peeling it)
1 cup (250 mL) raisins or other dried fruit

Apples make a perfect partner with oats, cinnamon, and raisins. These cookies are dense and chewy, some of the best oatmeal cookies I've ever had.

Preheat the oven to 350°F (180°C).

In a large bowl, beat the butter, oil, brown sugar, and cinnamon until creamy. Beat in the egg and vanilla.

Add the flour, oats, baking soda, and salt and stir until almost combined. Add the apple and raisins and stir just until blended.

Drop large spoonfuls onto a parchment-lined baking sheet and bake for 14 minutes or until set around the edges but still soft in the middle.

MAKES 1½–2 DOZEN COOKIES

apple browned butter blondies

½ cup (125 mL) butter
1 cup (250 mL) packed brown sugar
1 large egg
1 tsp (5 mL) vanilla or maple extract
1 cup (250 mL) all-purpose flour
½ tsp (2 mL) baking soda
¼ tsp (1 mL) salt
1 small or ½ large tart apple, cored and finely chopped
½ cup (125 mL) chopped pecans or walnuts

The brownie's lesser-known cousin is no less delicious, especially when made with browned butter, brown sugar, tart apple, and chopped pecans. Substitute a small, flavourful pear if you like.

Preheat the oven to 350°F (180°C).

In a small saucepan, melt the butter over medium-high heat. Keep it on the heat, swirling the pan occasionally, until the foam starts turning golden and the mixture smells nutty. Remove from heat and pour into a mixing bowl.

Stir in the brown sugar, then the egg and vanilla. Add the flour, baking soda, and salt and stir until almost combined. Add the apple and nuts and stir just until blended.

Spread into a greased or parchment-lined 8- × 8-inch (20 × 20 cm) pan and bake for 25–30 minutes, or until golden and just set. Cool in the pan on a wire rack.

MAKES 16 BLONDIES

cherry, white chocolate & pear biscotti

¾ cup (185 mL) brown sugar
1 very ripe pear, coarsely grated
2 large eggs
1 tsp (5 mL) vanilla
2½ cups (625 mL) all-purpose flour
1 tsp (5 mL) baking powder
1 tsp (5 mL) baking soda
¼ tsp (1 mL) salt
½ cup (125 mL) chopped white chocolate
⅓ cup (85 mL) dried cherries or cranberries

Pears are versatile, flavour-wise. They go well with white chocolate and dried cherries or cranberries, but you could also add chunks of dark chocolate, chopped candied ginger, cinnamon, and toasted walnuts—whatever inspires you.

Preheat the oven to 350°F (180°C).

In a large bowl, mix together the brown sugar, pear, eggs, and vanilla. In a smaller bowl, stir together the flour, baking powder, baking soda, and salt.

Add to the pear mixture and stir until almost combined. Add the chocolate and dried cherries or cranberries and stir just until blended.

On a parchment-lined baking sheet, shape the dough into a 14-inch- (35 cm) long log and flatten it until it's about 4 inches (10 cm) wide. (Alternatively, divide the dough in half and shape into two smaller logs for smaller biscotti.)

Bake for 30 minutes or until golden and set. Set aside to cool and reduce the oven temperature to 275°F (140°C).

Cut the log on a slight diagonal ½-inch (1 cm) thick, and place the slices upright back on the baking sheet. Bake for another hour, until golden, crisp, and dry. Turn the oven off, but leave the biscotti inside as it cools to harden further.

MAKES ABOUT 1½ DOZEN BISCOTTI

apple or pear fritters

½ cup (125 mL) all-purpose flour
¼ cup (60 mL) cornstarch
¼ tsp (1 mL) baking soda
¼ tsp (1 mL) cinnamon
1 cup (250 mL) milk or water
1–2 tart apples or ripe but firm pears
Canola oil, for frying
Icing sugar or cinnamon sugar, for sprinkling

Apples or pears sliced crosswise make rings that, when dipped in a thin batter, cook up to crisp, golden, doughnut-shaped fritters. Dust them with icing sugar or douse in cinnamon sugar and serve them warm.

In a medium bowl, whisk together the flour, cornstarch, baking soda, cinnamon, and enough milk or water to make a thin batter; it should have the consistency of thin cream.

Slice the apples or pears (don't bother peeling them) crosswise about ¼-inch (6 mm) thick and cut out the cores with the tip of a knife, making a ring.

In a wide pot, heat an inch or two (2.5–5 cm) of oil over medium-high heat until hot but not smoking. (You'll know it's ready when the oil bubbles around a scrap of bread held into it.) Dip a few slices of apple at a time into the batter, coating them completely, then gently slip into the oil. Cook a couple at a time for a minute or two, flipping with tongs as necessary, until golden. (If they're cooking too quickly, turn the heat down; if it's taking too long, the oil may need to be hotter. Don't crowd the pot, as this will bring the temperature of the oil down.)

Remove with a slotted spoon and transfer to paper towels to drain. Sprinkle with icing sugar or dip in a shallow dish of cinnamon sugar to coat while still warm.

MAKES ABOUT 2 DOZEN FRITTERS

maple-roasted apples

6 small, tart apples
½ cup (125 mL) chopped pecans
¼ cup (60 mL) raisins
1 tsp (5 mL) cinnamon
⅓ cup (85 mL) butter
⅓ cup (85 mL) pure maple syrup

A roasted (or baked) apple is the essence of pie without the pressure of pastry. It bakes in less time, so it can slide into the oven and make the house smell delicious as you enjoy dinner, emerging as a perfect vehicle for a scoop of vanilla ice cream.

Preheat the oven to 375°F (190°C).

Core the apples from the stem end using a sharp paring knife or a spoon, scooping them out while leaving ½ inch (1 cm) at the bottom. Divide the pecans and raisins between the apples, sprinkle each with a pinch of cinnamon, and dot each with butter. Place in a baking dish and drizzle the syrup overtop.

Add ½ cup (125 mL) warm water to the bottom of the baking dish and bake for 30–40 minutes, until the apples are tender.

Set each roasted apple on a plate, spoon the warm pan juices overtop, and serve with ice cream.

SERVES 6

braised cherry cheesecake in a jar

CRUST:
1 cup (250 mL) graham crumbs
2 Tbsp (30 mL) butter, melted

CHEESECAKE FILLING:
8 oz (250 g) package cream cheese, at room temperature
¼ cup (60 mL) sugar
½–¾ cup (125–185 mL) heavy (whipping) cream
¼ tsp (1 mL) vanilla

TOPPING:
2 cups (500 mL) fresh or frozen cherries, pitted
¼ cup (60 mL) sugar
¼ cup (60 mL) water

Individual cheesecakes in a jar are the perfect make-ahead dessert for a crowd. Keep them on ice with their lids on, and everyone can serve themselves when they're ready. Any soft, juicy stone fruit can be sliced and simmered with sugar into a chunky compote that's perfect for spooning overtop.

To make the crust, stir together the graham crumbs and melted butter. Divide between the bottoms of 6–8 small (½ cup/125 mL) ring-top jars.

In a medium bowl, beat the cream cheese, sugar, cream, and vanilla until smooth. Divide between the jars, spooning it over the crust.

To make the topping, bring the cherries, sugar, and water to a simmer in a medium saucepan. Cook for 10–15 minutes, until the cherries are soft, squishing some of them against the side of the pan with your spoon. Remove from heat and set aside to cool, then refrigerate until chilled.

Spoon the chilled topping over the cheesecakes. Screw on the lids and refrigerate until you're ready to serve them, or for up to 3 days.

MAKES 6–8 CHEESECAKES

pear sticky toffee pudding with cider sauce

- 1½ cups (375 mL) chopped, pitted dates
- 1 tsp (5 mL) baking soda
- ¼ cup (60 mL) butter, at room temperature
- 1 cup (250 mL) sugar
- 2 large eggs
- 1 tsp (5 mL) vanilla
- 2 cups (500 mL) all-purpose flour
- 1 tsp (5 mL) baking powder
- ¼ tsp (1 mL) salt
- 1 very ripe pear, coarsely grated

CIDER SAUCE:

- 1 cup (250 mL) apple cider
- 1 cup (250 mL) packed light brown sugar
- ½ cup (125 mL) heavy cream
- ¼ cup (60 mL) butter

Whipped cream or vanilla ice cream, for serving

A grated overripe pear provides moisture, sweetness, and an irresistible, slightly floral flavour to a classic sticky toffee pudding. This version is baked, so you don't have to worry about steaming it in a pudding mould. If you like, spike the toffee sauce with a shot of bourbon.

Preheat the oven to 350°F (180°C). In a medium saucepan, bring the dates to a simmer with 1¼ cups (310 mL) water. Remove from heat and stir in the baking soda. It will foam up, so make sure you have room. Pour into a bowl and set aside to cool.

In a large bowl, beat the butter and sugar together until sandy. Add the eggs and vanilla and beat until pale and light. In a small bowl, stir together the flour, baking powder, and salt. Add half the dry ingredients to the butter and sugar mixture and stir (or beat with a hand-held mixer on low) just until combined. Stir in the date mixture and pear, then the remaining dry ingredients, stirring just until blended.

Pour into a well-greased Bundt or similar-shaped pan and bake for 40–45 minutes, until deep golden, cracked on top, and springy to the touch. Let cool on a wire rack, then invert onto the rack or a plate while still slightly warm.

To make the sauce, bring the cider to a simmer in a medium saucepan and cook until it's reduced to about a quarter. Add the brown sugar, cream, and butter and bring to a simmer, whisking often. Remove from heat and set aside to cool.

Serve the cake topped with cider sauce and with whipped cream or ice cream.

SERVES 8

stone fruit pandowdy

1½–2 lb (750 g–1 kg) peaches, plums, cherries, or a combination
½ cup (125 mL) sugar, or to taste
1 Tbsp (15 mL) cornstarch
2 Tbsp (30 mL) butter
Pastry for a single-crust pie (see page 121; use one of the discs)
Milk and sugar, for brushing and sprinkling (optional)
Ice cream or whipped cream, for serving

A pandowdy is like a crisp, only with pastry on top instead of a crumble mixture. Often the pastry is laid overtop in patches; other times the baked pastry is broken with a spoon and pushed down into the bubbling juices, like crumbling crackers into soup.

Preheat the oven to 375°F (190°C).

In a baking dish or cast iron skillet, toss the fruit with the sugar and cornstarch. Spread out into a single layer and dot with butter.

On a lightly floured surface, roll out the pastry ¼-inch (6 mm) thick. Cut into shapes and lay over the fruit, overlapping slightly and mostly covering the fruit, but leaving some spaces for steam to escape. If you like, brush with milk and/or sprinkle with sugar.

Bake for 30 minutes or until the pastry is golden and the fruit is bubbly. Serve warm with ice cream or whipped cream.

SERVES 6

browned butter apricot cherry slump

- 6 apricots, pitted and thickly sliced
- 1 cup (250 mL) cherries, pitted and halved
- ¾ cup + 3 Tbsp (185 mL + 45 mL) sugar, divided, or to taste
- Pinch cinnamon
- ½ cup (125 mL) butter
- 2 large eggs
- 1 cup (250 mL) all-purpose flour
- Ice cream, whipped cream, or thick vanilla yogurt, for serving

A slump (also known as a grunt) is similar to a cobbler, with denser, more buttery cake batter poured overtop before baking. In this version the butter is browned first for a more intense, nutty flavour. It's far faster and easier to assemble than pie. Serve it warm with vanilla ice cream.

Preheat the oven to 350°F (180°C).

Toss the apricots and cherries in a buttered pie plate with 2 Tbsp (30 mL) sugar and the cinnamon.

In a small saucepan, melt the butter over medium heat. Keep cooking it, swirling the pan occasionally, for about 5 minutes or until it turns golden. Pour into a bowl.

Stir ¾ cup (185 mL) of sugar into the butter, then the eggs, then the flour. Spread over the fruit and sprinkle with the rest of the sugar.

Bake for 40–45 minutes, until golden and crusty and the juices are bubbling around the edges. Serve warm with vanilla ice cream, whipped cream, or thick vanilla yogurt.

SERVES 8

cherry clafoutis

3 large eggs
1 cup (250 mL) milk
½ cup (125 mL) sugar
2 tsp (10 mL) vanilla
½ cup (125 mL) all-purpose flour
¼ tsp (1 mL) salt
2 cups (500 mL) cherries, pitted
1 peach, sliced
Icing sugar, for dusting

Although cherry is traditional, this French country cross between a puffed pancake and custardy pudding can be made with virtually any kind of fruit—and juicy stone fruits like peaches, plums, and cherries tend to turn out very well.

Preheat the oven to 400°F (200°C) and butter a pie plate, gratin dish, or 9-inch (23 cm) cast iron skillet.

In a large bowl, whisk together the eggs, milk, sugar, and vanilla, or combine in a blender and pulse until smooth. Add the flour and salt and blend again until smooth.

Pour into the buttered dish and scatter with cherries and peach slices. Bake for 30 minutes, until slightly puffed and golden.

Sprinkle with icing sugar and serve warm, in wedges.

SERVES 8

peach, plum & cherry crumble

FRUIT BASE:

4 peaches, unpeeled
2 cups (500 mL) fresh or frozen cherries, pitted and halved
1 Tbsp (15 mL) cornstarch
½ cup (125 mL) sugar

CRUMBLE:

½ cup (125 mL) all-purpose flour
½ cup (125 mL) old-fashioned or quick oats
½ cup (125 mL) sugar (white or brown)
¼ cup (60 mL) butter
2 Tbsp (30 mL) honey or golden syrup

Ice cream, for serving

Stone fruits make the most delicious crumble. Feel free to substitute nectarines, apricots, or whatever's in season. Leftovers are delicious the next morning for breakfast served with thick plain or vanilla yogurt.

Preheat the oven to 350°F (180°C).

Thickly slice the peaches into a pie plate or shallow baking dish, then add the cherries. In a small dish or measuring cup, stir the cornstarch into the sugar and sprinkle it over the fruit; toss gently to combine.

In a bowl (or the bowl of a food processor), combine the crumble ingredients and blend with a fork (or pulse in the processor) until well blended and sticky/crumbly. Sprinkle the crumble over the fruit, squeezing it as you go to create larger clumps.

Bake for 40–45 minutes, until golden and the fruit is tender and bubbly around the edges.

Serve warm with ice cream.

SERVES 6

roasted plum, apricot, or peach ice cream

4–6 large plums or apricots or 2–3 peaches, halved and pitted
Sugar, for sprinkling
1 cup (250 mL) good-quality plain yogurt or sour cream
1 cup (250 mL) heavy (whipping) cream
½ cup (125 mL) sugar, or to taste

Roasting stone fruit softens it, releasing its juices and intensifying its flavour. Soft, roasted fruit is perfect for swirling into ice cream; try roasted peaches with sour cream or roasted plum with yogurt.

Preheat the oven to 400°F (200°C).

Place the halved plums, apricots, or peaches cut side up on a parchment-lined rimmed baking sheet and sprinkle with sugar. Roast for about 20 minutes, until the fruit softens, releases some juice, and turns golden and sticky. Set aside to cool.

In a bowl, whisk together the yogurt or sour cream, cream, and sugar or honey. Freeze in your ice cream machine according to the manufacturer's directions.

Meanwhile, scrape the roasted fruit (along with any juices or stickiness left on the bottom of the pan) into a food processor and pulse until coarsely chopped. Alternatively, chop the fruit roughly with a knife on a chopping board that will catch all the juices. Make sure the fruit is completely cool; if it's still warm, it could melt the ice cream.

When the ice cream is frozen but still soft, add the roasted fruit through the feed tube or stir it in. Serve immediately or transfer to a container and freeze until solid.

MAKES ABOUT 4 CUPS (1 L)

PRESERVES

ginger peach skillet jam

4 ripe peaches
½–1 cup (125–250 mL) packed brown sugar
2 tsp (10 mL) grated fresh ginger
1 Tbsp (15 mL) lemon juice

A single batch of peach preserves cook up quickly in a skillet, which has a larger surface area. Brown sugar adds a caramel flavour, the ginger a peppery warmth.

To peel the peaches, drop them into a pot of boiling water. Remove after a minute (use tongs or a slotted spoon) and plunge into a bowl of ice water to stop them from cooking. Once cool enough to handle, slip off the skins with your fingers.

In a bowl, roughly mash your peaches with a fork or potato masher, or if they're ripe enough, simply squeeze them with your fingers into a large, heavy skillet. Set it over medium-high heat and stir in the sugar, ginger, and lemon juice.

Cook, stirring often, until the mixture bubbles and the fruit softens. Simmer for 20 minutes or until it thickens enough that your spoon leaves a trail through the jam. Remove from heat, pour into a jar or bowl, and cool completely.

MAKES ABOUT 1½ CUPS (375 ML)

cider plum jam

- 2 lb (1 kg) plums, pitted and coarsely chopped
- 1 large tart apple, coarsely grated, or 2 apricots, pitted and coarsely chopped
- 1 cup (250 mL) cider or water
- 3 cups (750 mL) sugar
- 2 Tbsp (30 mL) lemon juice

Apple cider contains lots of pectin, so it helps plum jam to gel while adding sweetness and flavour. Use any kind of plums you like, or a combination—or try mixing plums and apricots.

Put a small saucer into the freezer to chill to test the jam.

In a medium pot, combine the plums, apple, and cider or water and bring to a simmer; cook for 20 minutes, until the fruit is very soft.

Add the sugar and lemon juice and bring back to a simmer. Cook for 20–30 minutes, until thick and jam-like. If you drop a small spoonful onto the cold saucer from the freezer, the jam should wrinkle when you push it with your finger. If not, keep simmering until it sets.

Cool and refrigerate for up to a month, or freeze for up to 6 months.

MAKES ABOUT 5 CUPS (1.25 L)

apple peach barbecue sauce

- 1–2 apples, pears, or peaches, peeled, cored or pitted, and chopped, or 3–4 plums or 2 cups (500 mL) cherries, pitted and finely chopped, or a combination
- ¼ cup (60 mL) coarsely grated or finely chopped red onion
- 1¼ cups (310 mL) ketchup
- ½ cup (125 mL) apple cider vinegar
- ⅓ cup (85 mL) packed brown sugar
- 1 Tbsp (15 mL) grainy mustard
- 1 garlic clove, finely crushed or grated
- Freshly ground black pepper

Apples, pears, and soft stone fruits like peaches, nectarines, or even plums and cherries work well in homemade barbecue sauce, lending sweetness and tang. Use them together in any combination. Cook down the fruit first, then mash it before adding the remaining ingredients. If you include the skin, make sure you chop the fruit finely. If you like, add a shot of bourbon to the mix.

Place the chopped fruit in a medium saucepan along with the onion and add just enough water to cover. Bring to a simmer and cook for 20–30 minutes, until very soft. Mash with a potato masher.

Add the ketchup, vinegar, brown sugar, mustard, garlic, and pepper and bring to a simmer. Cook, stirring often, for 20 minutes or until thickened.

Use immediately, or cool and store in the fridge for up to a month or in the freezer for up to 6 months.

MAKES ABOUT 2½ CUPS (625 ML)

all-fruit mincemeat

- 2 apples, coarsely grated
- 2 pears, cored and finely chopped
- Grated zest and juice of 1 lemon
- Grated zest and juice of 1 orange
- 1 cup (250 mL) dried cherries or 2 cups (500 mL) fresh cherries, pitted and chopped
- 1 cup (250 mL) raisins
- 1 cup (250 mL) golden raisins
- ½ cup (125 mL) dried or 1 cup (250 mL) fresh apricots, chopped
- ½ cup (125 mL) candied citron or peel
- 1½ cups (375 mL) dark brown sugar
- ¼ cup (60 mL) butter
- 1–2 cinnamon sticks
- 1 tsp (5 mL) cinnamon or pumpkin pie spice
- Pinch salt
- ½ cup (125 mL) chopped walnuts or pecans, toasted (optional)

In fall, making a big batch of fruity mincemeat with apples and pears at their peak is the perfect way to preserve them for the upcoming holiday season. Cherries make a delicious addition, as do dried or fresh apricots.

In a large saucepan, combine all the ingredients except the walnuts or pecans (if you're using them) over medium-high heat.

Bring to a simmer and cook, stirring often, for 20–30 minutes, until dark golden and thick. Remove from heat and let cool; stir in the nuts if using them.

Store in a sealed container or jars in the fridge for up to 2 weeks, or freeze for 6 months.

MAKES ABOUT 4 CUPS (1 L), ENOUGH FOR TWO PIES OR A FEW DOZEN TARTS

cranberry pear ginger preserves

- 5–6 ripe pears, cored and roughly chopped
- 1½ cups (375 mL) sugar
- 1 cup (250 mL) apple cider
- 1 Tbsp (15 mL) grated fresh ginger
- 1–2 cups (250–500 mL) fresh or frozen cranberries or cherries

These chunky, not-too-sweet preserves are easier to make than most. The pears make this more like a chunky sauce than gelled jam, but it's sweet enough to act like a preserve, perfect for spreading on toast or biscuits.

Combine all the ingredients in a large pot and bring to a simmer over medium-high heat. Reduce heat and cook, occasionally mashing with a large spoon or potato masher, until the mixture thickens and looks more uniform and jam-like. It will thicken further as it cools.

Transfer to clean jars and refrigerate for up to a month, or freeze for up to 6 months.

MAKES 3–4 CUPS (750 ML–1 L)

peach & plum ketchup

Canola oil, for cooking
1 small onion, finely chopped
2 garlic cloves, crushed
2 tsp (10 mL) grated fresh ginger
2 Tbsp (30 mL) tomato paste or ¼ cup (60 mL) tomato sauce
½ tsp (2 mL) curry powder or paste
¼ tsp (1 mL) cinnamon
¼ cup (60 mL) white balsamic or white wine vinegar
4 large peaches, pitted and chopped
2–3 plums, pitted and chopped
⅓ cup (85 mL) packed brown sugar
Salt, to taste

Tomatoes don't have the monopoly on ketchup. Ripe peaches and plums make sweet, tart, perfectly acidic "ketchup" that's reminiscent of chutney. It's a perfect condiment for curries, samosas, and roast chicken sandwiches—even burgers.

In a large saucepan, heat a drizzle of oil over medium-high heat and sauté the onion for 3–4 minutes, until soft. Add the garlic and ginger and cook for another minute.

Add the tomato paste or sauce, curry powder or paste, and cinnamon and cook for another minute. Add the vinegar and cook until it reduces by about half, then add the peaches, plums, brown sugar, and a pinch of salt.

Reduce the heat and simmer for about 15 minutes, until the fruit is very soft. Remove from heat and purée with a hand-held immersion blender right in the pot, or carefully transfer to a blender or food processor and pulse until smooth.

Store in jars in the fridge for up to a month or the freezer for up to 6 months.

MAKES ABOUT 2 CUPS (500 ML)

apple & pear chutney

- 3 tart apples, cored and chopped
- 2 ripe but firm pears, cored and chopped
- 1 small onion, finely chopped
- 1 small red pepper, finely chopped
- 2 cups (500 mL) packed brown sugar
- ½ cup (125 mL) raisins
- ¾ cup (185 mL) apple cider vinegar
- Finely grated zest and juice of 1 lemon
- 1 Tbsp (15 mL) grainy mustard
- ½ tsp (2 mL) curry powder or paste
- ½ tsp (2 mL) salt

Apples and pears make a delicious chutney; it's a great way to preserve the best of the season. Serve it with roast ham, chicken, or turkey, or with curries or samosas.

Combine all the ingredients in a medium pot set over medium-high heat. Bring to a simmer and cook, stirring often, for 45 minutes to an hour, until the apples and pears are tender and the mixture has thickened.

Cool and divide into containers or jars and refrigerate for up to a month, or freeze for up to 6 months.

MAKES 5–6 CUPS (1.25–1.5 L)

peach or apricot chutney

- 2 lb (1 kg) peaches, nectarines, or apricots, or a combination (about 6 pieces of fruit)
- 1 small onion, finely chopped
- 1–2 garlic cloves, crushed
- 1 Tbsp (15 mL) grated fresh ginger
- 1 jalapeño pepper, seeded and minced
- ½ red bell pepper, seeded and finely chopped
- 1 cup (250 mL) packed brown sugar
- ½ cup (125 mL) apple cider or rice vinegar
- ¼ tsp (1 mL) salt
- Pinch red pepper flakes

Use peaches, nectarines, or apricots for this tangy-sweet chutney. Reminiscent of classic mango chutney, it's perfect with curries, samosas, or roast chicken or pork, on sandwiches, or alongside cheese platters.

To peel the peaches, nectarines, or apricots, drop a few at a time into a pot of boiling water. Remove after a minute (use tongs or a slotted spoon) and plunge into a bowl of ice water to stop them from cooking. Once cool enough to handle, slip off the skins with your fingers. Halve the fruit, pit them, and roughly chop them, reserving any juices that accumulate.

Put the chopped fruit (and juices) into a medium pot and add the remaining ingredients. Bring to a boil over medium-high heat and simmer for about 20 minutes, stirring often, until the fruit softens and the mixture thickens. Continue to cook if it seems too runny, keeping in mind it will thicken further as it cools. Remove from heat and cool completely.

Divide into containers and refrigerate for up to a month, or freeze for up to 6 months.

MAKES 6–8 CUPS (1.5–2 L)

ACKNOWLEDGEMENTS

Huge thanks to everyone who helped bring this book to life: the brilliant and oh-so-lovely Taryn Boyd, who shared my vision of bringing the fruits of the Okanagan to peoples' homes and kitchens; to Pete, Renée, and Tori at Touchwood Editions for designing, editing, and getting this book out there, and for being so patient with me and altogether fantastic to work with. Thanks to Lana for editing, and Shallon of Salt Food Photography for the stunning cover. Also, a big thanks to Chris Pollock from BC Tree Fruits for supporting this project, and to all the growers and their families throughout the Okanagan for all you bring to our table. And thanks to my family, particularly Mike and Willem, for being testers—and even eating the duds.

INDEX

TouchWood Editions
touchwoodeditions.com

LIBRARY AND ARCHIVES CANADA CATALOGUING IN PUBLICATION
Van Rosendaal, Julie, 1970–. Author
Out of the orchard : recipes for fresh fruit from the sunny Okanagan / Julie Van Rosendaal.

Issued in print and electronic formats.
ISBN 978-1-77151-132-2

1. Cooking (Fruit)—British Columbia—Okanagan Valley (Region).
2. Cooking, Canadian—British Columbia style. 3. Cookbooks. I. Title.

TX811.V35 2016 641.6'4 C2015-908779-1

Editor: Lana Okerlund
Designer: Pete Kohut
Food photography: Julie Van Rosendaal
All other interior images: BC Tree Fruits

We acknowledge the financial support of the Government of Canada through the Canada Book Fund and the province of British Columbia through the Book Publishing Tax Credit.

Nous reconnaissons l'aide financière du gouvernement du Canada par l'entremise du Fonds du livre du Canada et la province de la Colombie-Britannique par le Crédit d'impôt pour l'édition de livres.

This book was produced using FSC®-certified, acid-free papers, processed chlorine free, and printed with soya-based inks.

1 2 3 4 5 20 19 18 17 16

PRINTED IN CHINA